Publications of the
Institute of Germanic Studies
Volume 15

ESSAYS IN
GERMAN AND DUTCH LITERATURE

ESSAYS IN GERMAN AND DUTCH LITERATURE

Edited by

W. D. ROBSON-SCOTT

Honorary Director of the Institute of Germanic Studies

INSTITUTE OF GERMANIC STUDIES
UNIVERSITY OF LONDON
1973

International Standard Book no. 0 85457 051 9

PRINTED BY W. S. MANEY AND SON LTD LEEDS LS9 7DL ENGLAND

Contents

Preface

THIS VOLUME consists of a selection of papers read to the Institute between November 1969 and May 1972. It is thus a belated sequel to *Essays in German Literature — I*, edited by Frederick Norman (Institute Publication No. 7) in 1965. In the preface to that collection Professor Norman stated that it was intended to publish further volumes of miscellaneous essays at intervals of not more than two years, but in fact no such volume appeared until *Essays in German Language, Culture and Society*, edited by S. S. Prawer, R. Hinton Thomas, and Leonard Forster, in 1969. And this volume was different in character from *Essays in German Literature — I*, in that it consisted of essays specially written for the volume, none of which had been delivered at the Institute.

This volume differs from its predecessor, *Essays in German Literature — I* in two respects: first, it consists solely of papers read to the Institute, whereas the former volume also contained addresses delivered to the Conference of University Teachers of German in Great Britain and Ireland; secondly, the contents of this volume are not confined specifically to German Literature; we are particularly glad to be able to include a contribution by Professor Weevers, for many years Professor of Dutch Language and Literature in the University of London.

I should like to express the hope that Professor Norman's original intention will be carried out, and that collections of miscellaneous essays, consisting of papers delivered to the Institute, will be published at regular intervals in future.

W. D. ROBSON-SCOTT

Marvels of the East in the *Wiener Genesis* and in Wolfram's *Parzival* [1]

By R. A. WISBEY

FOR THE poet of the *Wiener Genesis*,[2] the fabulous peoples of the East can be traced back to the disobedience of Adam's progeny:

> 646 Adam hiez si mîden wurze,   daz si inen
> newurren an ir geburte.
> sîn gebot si verchurn,   ir geburt si flurn.

(*Millstätter Genesis*, ed. J. Diemer, 26.2: daz si si niht entarten   an der ir geburte.) This characteristically terse, almost perfunctory aside has never been adequately clarified.[3] It is tempting to look no further for an explanation than the abundant support offered by learned or folk medicine and superstition for the beneficial or maleficent effects of herbs and roots, not least in the sexual sphere.[4] Medicinal treatises containing sections *De virtutibus quarundam herbarum vel radicum* are widespread in Latin and are accessible in German by the twelfth century.[5] In *Reinfrid von Braunschweig* (*c.* 1300, ed. K. Bartsch), the origin of the monstrous peoples is likewise traced back to disregard of Adam's instructions, but this time the view advanced without commentary in the *Wiener Genesis* is elaborated by elements drawn from the common stock of medicinal knowledge. Some herbs are poisonous, some fortify the body, others either heighten fertility or counteract it. After considering two herbs, one which prevents and another which procures miscarriage,[6] the author of *Reinfrid* goes on to a third:

> 19725 sô hât daz dritte lîht die art,
> swer ez nôz, daz dâ von wart
> daz ungeborne kint ein tier,
> wan sîn kraft diu bôt im schier
> ein unmenschlîch figûre.
> nâ der wurz nâtûre
> wart einez sus, daz ander sô.

Adam possessed this knowledge in its entirety:

> 19710 sîn hôher meisterlîcher list
> marht und bekande alle maht,
> der wurzen und der kriuter kraft . . .
> als im nâtûre helfe bôt.

Whether Adam's warning to avoid corruption of their human form (19734 f.) was heeded by his children in the generations before the Flood *Reinfrid* does not reveal.

In the light of this passage it may seem idle to probe further into the statement of the *Wiener Genesis* quoted at the outset. After all, the knowledge implicitly attributed to Adam might be felt to constitute hardly more than a natural inference from the fact that, in Paradise before the Fall, he was surrounded by plants and herbs, the luxuriance and healing power of which is a commonplace of Genesis commentary.[7] One may add that the interpretation *ad litteram* of Genesis 1. 29 f.: 'Ecce dedi vobis omnem herbam afferentem semen super terram, et universa ligna . . . ut sint vobis in escam, et cunctis animantibus terræ' gives rise to the belief that Adam, together with all the animals, were vegetarians until the Fall — according to some accounts, until after the Flood.[8] John Chrysostom asks how one could reasonably assume (*Homiliæ in Genesim*, PG 53, 132,6, with Latin translation), that Adam, who, already before he tasted the forbidden fruit 'tanta sapientia plenus erat, et cum scientia etiam prophetica gratia dignatus est', lacked knowledge of good and evil, when even sheep and goats could distinguish edible plants from noxious ('quæ herba sit salutaris, et cibo utilis, et quæ perniciosa, ut illam adeat, hanc studiose fugiat').

Precisely that discrimination which John Chrysostom accords to the pre-lapsarian Adam is attributed to the fallen Adam in a passage of the German *Lucidarius*, long recognized by scholarship as closely related to the accounts in the *Wiener Genesis* and in *Parzival*:[9]

Der meister sprach: 'Adam was der wiseste man der ie geborn wart. do er uz dem paradiso cam, do ercander die wurzen alle. die der nature warent, swel wib die eze, daz die geburt da von verwandelt wurde, do warnete er sine dothere daz si der wurze nith ezen. do ge*wunnen* dú wip vírwiz wie ez umbe die wurze stûende die in ir vatir hete verboten. die kint die von den wurden geborn, die verwandeltin sich nach den wurzen unde misserietent . . .'

(ed. F. Heidlauf, p. 12, 26 ff.). The established sources of the *Lucidarius* provide no better guide to the exact provenance of these statements about Adam's specialist knowledge, and its application, than do those of the *Wiener Genesis*.[10] The corresponding lines of *Parzival*, which can thus derive only in part from the earlier encyclopaedic work, place the wisdom of Adam in a much wider setting. Unequivocally, Adam is seen as possessing 'kunst' bestowed by God before the Fall: this applies no less to his astronomical knowledge, introduced here by Wolfram, and — to judge from the parallelism 'er rekant . . . er rekant' — also to his recognition of the nature and 'virtues' of each individual herb:[11]

> 518.1 Unser vater Adâm,
> die kunst er von gote nam,

er gap allen dingen namn,
beidiu wilden unde zamn:
er rekant ouch ieslîches art,
dar zuo der sterne umbevart,
der siben plânêten,
waz die krefte hêten:
er rekant ouch aller würze maht,
und waz ieslîcher was geslaht.

(ed. K. Lachmann, fifth edition, 1947)

As D. A. Wells has shown, this passage derives ultimately from a ramified and impressive tradition of
Hebrew (or, indirectly, Babylonian) origin.[12] Here we
must reckon with the influence of pseudepigraphic
literature as well as with mediation by the writings of
Philo of Alexandria. Origen, Eusebius, Ephraem, and
Jerome are known to have been tutored by Rabbis, while
Tertullian, Lactantius, Ambrose and even Augustine
consulted Jewish scholars in the course of their studies of
the Bible. 'Many a Haggadah first met with in Jewish
literature in a Midrash composed in the seventh or
eighth century, and even later, was transmitted as Jewish
tradition by the Church Fathers of the fifth or fourth
or even the third century' (Ginzberg, The Legends of the
Jews, v, ix). In such sources Adam is seen in paradise
as the homo caelestis,[13] possessed of giant yet perfect
stature, his countenance radiant with divine beauty,[14]
endowed with a wisdom exceeding even that of the
angels. This latter belief rested not least on his ability to
name the animals according to their natures (Gen.
II. 19–20),[15] an ability to which Wolfram also refers (see
above). According to the Hexaemeron of the Venerable
Bede, the name of Adam, in accordance with his creation
from earth (earth taken from the four quarters, as some
sources[16] add), is composed of the initial letters of the

Greek terms for the four regions of the world: 'A, et D, et A, et M, a quibus litteris et quatuor orbis plagæ, cum Græce nominantur, initium sumunt. Vocatur namque apud eos anatole oriens, dysis occidens, arctos septentrio, mesembria meridies' (PL 91, 78C). This notion, also present in Irish exegesis,[17] which, like early Irish literature, is strikingly receptive to apocryphal material,[18] is also found in the Second Book of Enoch (The Book of the Secrets of Enoch). The main body of this work, which is preserved only in late Slavonic MSS, goes back to a lost Greek original, of either Jewish-Christian or of purely Christian origin. The extracts cited below represent material probably interpolated into the shorter Slavonic version (tenth or eleventh century) after 1250, from an unknown source or sources combining ancient elements[19] — our third quotation from it derives indirectly from Gregory of Nazianzus (PG 36, 321, cf. 631; Vaillant, p. 101). In their juxtaposition these passages provide evidence of a cohesive and persistent apocryphal tradition concerning the cosmic nature and status of Adam. Describing the sixth day of Creation 2 Enoch reads: 'And I appointed him a name, from the four component parts, from east, from west, from south, from north, and I appointed for him four special stars, and I called his name Adam, and showed him the two ways, the light and the darkness, and I told him: "This is good and that bad" ' (ed. Charles, II, 449).

The preceding section is among the best known of the widespread portrayals of Adam (and therefore of man) as microcosm, a notion familiar to certain Early Middle High German religious poets and to Wolfram,[20] and which, in this form, again could have entered the vernacular literatures of western Europe through the mediation of Ireland. Despite certain divergences the

affinity of, for instance, the *Ezzolied* (Vorau version) 5,
3 ff. with 2 Enoch is unmistakable:

> von dem leime gab er ime daz fleisch,   der tow
>   becechenit den sweiz,
> von dem steine gab er ime daz pein . . .

'On the sixth day I commanded my wisdom to create man
from seven consistencies: one, his flesh from the earth;
two, his blood from the dew; three, his eyes from the
sun; four, his bones from stone; five, his intelligence from
the swiftness of the angels and from cloud; six, his veins
and his hair from the grass of the earth; seven, his soul
from my breath and from the wind' (Charles, II, 448 f.).[21]
Even more significant in our present context is what
follows:[22] 'I created man from invisible and from visible
nature, of both are his death and life and image, he knows
speech like some created thing, small in greatness and
again great in smallness, and I placed him on earth, a
second angel, honourable, great and glorious, and I
appointed him as ruler to rule on earth and to have my
wisdom, and there was none like him of earth of all my
existing creatures' (Charles, II, 449). Even this does not
exhaust the importance of this section from 2 Enoch for
our purpose, for it describes how, on the fourth day of
creation God orders the heavens, determining the posi-
tions of the seven named planets, and fixing the sun's
path through the zodiac. A precipitate of such traditions
concerning the universal wisdom and cosmic affinities of
Adam is found not only in vernacular literature, for
example in Wolfram, but also in Christian iconography:
in the *Hortus deliciarum*, fol. 16, the seven planets form a
halo round the head of the microcosmic *homo coelestis*,
while in other depictions Adam is surrounded by the
signs of the zodiac.[23]

The statement in Gen. v. 1: 'Hoc est liber generationis Adam' comes to be interpreted as proof that God laid before the patriarch a book in which the genealogy of the whole human race was recorded.[24] It is presumably this idea, underlined by the so-called *Testament of Adam*, which gives rise to the view that Adam possessed prophetic gifts; this we encountered in the quotation from Chrysostom cited earlier. According to the *Zohar*, which originated in the thirteenth century but which rests on older material, a book presented to Adam by an angel conveys revelations concerning 72 types of wisdom.[25] Apocryphal, patristic and medieval sources contain frequent references to individual skills of Adam besides those already mentioned. The authorship of lapidaries, for example, could be attributed to Adam or to Enoch.[26] Wolfram is surely transcending the purely formulaic when he alludes to wise Pictagoras:

> 773.26   der ein astronomierre[27] was,
> und sô wîse âne strît,
> niemen sît Adâmes zît
> möhte im glîchen sin getragen.
> der kunde wol von steinen sagen . . .

Occasionally, too, Adam is recognized as the founder of other liberal arts,[28] and of the technique of writing, a view put forward by apocryphal sources, but also by Augustine.[29] In an episode from the *Vita Adae et Evae*, again of Jewish origin, but existing in Latin from the fourth century,[30] God has the Archangel Michael take seeds to Adam and show him how to till the ground,[31] while in the related *Apocalypsis Mosis*, Adam beseeches God for permission to take away with him from Paradise fragrant herbs for sacrifice — he is also allowed seeds for planting: here again Adam becomes the initiator of human activities and skills.

The *Vita Adae*, a German prose version of which is preserved in a manuscript of the fifteenth century, was certainly known in Germany much earlier.[32] *Reinfrid* at first sight appears to provide evidence of this when it portrays the concern of wise men living immediately before the deluge lest all the knowledge gained by mankind should perish in the cataclysm prophesied by Adam. A solution is found in the erection of two pillars with inscriptions, one of 'liehtem marmelsteine' (19784) to survive a Flood, the other 'von gebranter ziegel pfliht' to withstand destruction by fire. This narration, however, does not stem directly from the *Vita Adae*, which contains an alternative version — Eve exhorts the sons and daughters of Adam to make two *tables* in order to record the deeds of their parents[33] — but, probably via the *Historia Scholastica* (PL 198, 1079B), from the *Jewish Antiquities* of Josephus (1, 70–1). The Latin translation of this work, produced in the circle of Cassiodorus in the late sixth century, became one of the most popular school-books of the Middle Ages, and is extant in over 200 manuscripts.[34] *Reinfrid* reports how the pillars were discovered after the deluge and how women were intrigued by a rumour that the inscriptions described the baleful effects of herbs:

> 19833   dô wâren sî sô niugern
> daz ir sin niht wolt enbern,
> sî wolten sîn geruochen
> und endelîch versuochen
> ob ez alsô wære.

From this womanly *curiositas*, according to some authorities precisely the vice which had led to the Fall,[35] resulted the misshapen creatures discussed earlier, 'frömde figûre', whose nature 'von menschlîcher wildet'. Here the poet is obviously concerned, like Augustine (*De Civitate*

Dei, XVI, 8), not only with the question of whether such monsters were human or animal, but also with the problem of their existence after the Flood, a difficulty which neither the *Wiener Genesis* nor Wolfram resolves or even faces up to, and which cannot concern us here, save in passing. We may note, however, that in the Book of Jubilees 8, 1 ff. (Charles, II, p. 25), a descendant of Noah is led into sin by inscriptions which former generations have carved on rock and which have thus survived the Flood.[36] It seems possible that the legend of Noah was older than that of Enoch and that 'the latter was built up on the débris of the former' (Charles, II, p. 168).

While we have succeeded to some extent in illuminating in a general way the traditions underlying the Middle High German passages discussed so far, we have not unearthed an exact source for the warning of Adam to his children, even in the Jewish legends of Adam.[37] Before proceeding, however, we should note that this motif is also preserved in a manuscript of *c*. 1300 known as the *Rothschild Canticles*. Here Adam addresses his daughters at Damascus and tells them that if they eat certain herbs ('diverse herbe de natura speciali') they will conceive monsters such as humans with the necks and heads of cranes, dog-headed men, skiapods, centaurs, cyclopes, men with long pendant ears or with a monkey's head.[38] The wording of the prohibition in the *Canticles* and the disregard of it accords well with that in the *Wiener Genesis*, the *Lucidarius*, Wolfram and *Reinfrid* ('Adam prohibuit omnibus filiabus suis ne comederent ab illa herba ac tamen comederunt'), as does the accompanying reference to the knowledge of Adam: ('Adam scientiam omnium herbarum et omnium rerum [possedebat]') — he is also said to be seven times wiser than Solomon, seven times fairer than Absalom, seven times stronger than Samson. Janson, who

2

is not aware of the German parallels considered above, postulates an Early Christian origin for this legend (p. 95). On the other hand the nature of the comparison with other Old Testament figures suggests a Jewish origin.[39] There may be a hint of influence by the German *Lucidarius*, or a dependent source, in the fact that in the relatively late *Canticles* manuscript a section drawn from the *Elucidarium* of Honorius of Autun closely follows the chapter on monsters.[40]

Until such time as an apocryphal or other source can be adduced, this theme must therefore be regarded as a separate development for which the *Wiener Genesis* provides the first evidence.[41] It is important to note this fact, since the genesis of the fabulous creatures of the East is often explained — when any explanation is attempted — within the framework of the legend of Cain.[42] In this the *Wiener Genesis* is no exception. During my earlier dis-discussion of the progeny of Adam I resorted to a narrative device beloved of Wolfram, deliberately with-holding until 'her nâch sô des wirdet zît' (*Parz.*, 241.5) the information that the *Wiener Genesis* is referring here more specifically to the descendants of Cain:

> 644   duo wurten die scuzlinge   glîch deme stamme:
> ubel wuocher si bâren,   dem tivele vageten.
>
> Adam hiez si mîden wurze . . .

The poet seizes the opportunity, as he does when com-menting on the Fall (505 ff.), of establishing a tropo-logical link with the present: Cain taught his children 'dei zouber dei hiute sint' (643, including the misuse of herbs 645 ?). They were thus subject to the devil. Cain is engendered by Adam (Gen. IV.1), but while Seth and his descendants earn the 'tiuren miltnamen' of 'children of God' they are, by this very fact, 'von Kaînes chinden

gesceiden. / der vater hiez Belial, daz ist der leidige
tiefal . . .' (666 f.). In the context this can only be understood in a spiritual sense, although the poet was perhaps
acquainted with a Jewish tradition, known to Irenaeus,
Hippolytus, and Epiphanius among others, according to
which Eve succumbed to the physical blandishments of
Satan, so that Cain was quite literally the son of the devil.
This view rested first and foremost on a literal interpretation of the First Epistle of St John iii. 12: 'Non
sicut Cain, qui ex maligno erat . . .'.[43]

In the *Wiener Genesis*, as in Genesis iv. 1 ff., the first
action of Adam and Eve after being cast out of Paradise is
intercourse and its consequence is the conception of Cain.
This sorry event provokes the author to a passionate and
highly stylized reflexion on man's fallen state (539 ff.).
An accumulation of conditional clauses and an intense
concentration of key words, lead on to several short half-
lines of breathless urgency, resolved eventually in the
assurance, voiced several times since the Fall, but here
repeated for the last time, that repentance would have
brought God's forgiveness, even at this late hour:

546   jâ wâre sô michel sîn gnâde   daz dar an newâre
                    nehein twâla
            er nehête in iz fergeben . . .

Then, as so often in the work, the tropological concern
for the present reasserts itself, revealing criticism of
others as self-indulgence:

548   Gnuoch haben wir in ferwizen,   wolte wir
              unsech selben dâ bî bezzeren!

In this excursus, its impact heightened by anaphora,
parallelism, repetition, variation and other devices of
Christian rhetoric,[44] in an elevated style applied here to a
highly appropriate subject, the poet prepares the hearer

for a world in which, after the birth of Cain, the bridge
to a paradisaic present is finally torn down. From this
moment onwards hope lies only in the future achievement
of a heavenly paradise by way of contrition and penance,
as is made abundantly plain in the scene where God
observes Cain's wrath against Abel, and leaves to him the
choice between good and evil:

> 620   'Wil dû wol tuon,   des vindestû lôn;
> hâst anderes gedâht,   des wirt ouch rât.
> ich lâzze dir den zugel   ze tuonne guot oder ubel.
> alsô dich gezimet   den ent ez genimet.'

Cain and Abel, however, are 'mit ungelichem willen'.
After the murder of his brother, Cain's total unwilling-
ness to seek God's forgiveness leads him to become
the type of the unrepentant sinner: 'sîn buoze newas
porguot,   ubel was sîn herze jouch sîn muot' (642). With
this we have returned to the progeny of Cain, whose
impious upbringing culminates in offences of their own,
and in their misshapen offspring. In them, too, a false
direction of the human will proves decisive: 'die after-
chomen an in zeigtun   was ir vorderen garnet hêten'
(659).

For his description of these fabulous creatures the poet
of the *Wiener Genesis* does not resort directly to classical
sources, like the *Natural History* of Pliny the Elder,
but to such dependent authorities as the *Etymologies*
of Isidor (xi.3 'De Portentis'),[45] or to the exact reproduction of this account in the *De Universo* by Rabanus (vii.7:
PL 111, 195C ff.). Apart from the unusual explanation
'Adam hiez si mîden wurze' the originality of the poet
consists here above all in his selection of motifs and in
his treatment of them. Although Adam is inwardly
corrupted by the Fall, his flesh still reflects his creation

in the image of God. But with the action of Cain and his daughters, the integrity of man's outward appearance is destroyed in a second Fall clearly set in parallel to the first,[46] and is replaced by a diversity of forms externalizing the chaos of sin:

> 648 dei chint si gebâren   dei unglîch wâren . . .
> 660 alsolich si wâren innen,   solich wurten dise ûzzen.

The examples selected by the poet do not stem from Isidor's comments on deformed individuals, however, but are representative of the monstrous races:[47] 'Sicut autem in singulis gentibus quaedam monstra sunt hominum, ita in universo genere humano quaedam monstra sunt gentium, ut Gigantes, Cynocephali, Cyclopes et cetera' (*Etym.*, xi.3, 12). As we have already noted, the poet is preoccupied here with the corruption of man's physical nature, which had been created by God to reflect the divine order, and thus concerns himself particularly with those capacities which render man specifically human, like sight 'daz er sehe die getougen' (121), the gift of language (127) and his upright gait:[48]

> 104 'Er sol uns sîn gelîch,   aller gescepfte forhtlîch.
> ûfreht sol er gên,   an zwein beinen stên,
> daz er ze himele warte,   merche der sternen geverte,
> merch iegelich zît   an deme himele wît.'

The ninth-century *Epistola de Cynocephalis* by Ratramnus maintains: 'Hominum . . . est rotundum vertice cœlum aspicere, canum vero oblongo capite rostroque deducto terram intueri. Et homines loquuntur, canes vere latrant' (PL 121, 1153C f.). As in his description of the creation of man (115 ff.) the poet of the *Wiener Genesis* begins with the head, so too here he begins with the corruption of man's countenance, and with the displacement of the organs of sight and speech. Then he

proceeds to monsters with misshapen feet and to others
which go on all fours like beasts, concluding, as at the
creation of Adam (199), with the skin. In certain races this
has ceased to reflect the radiance of its divine origin
(cf. *Parzival*, 123.16 f.: 'nie mannes varwe baz geriet /
vor im sît Adâmes zît') and they have taken on animal
character:

> 649   sumeliche hêten houbet sam hunt;   sumeliche
> hêten an den brusten den munt,
> an den ahselun dei ougen,   dei muosen sich des
> houbtes gelouben . . .
>
> Etlicher hêt einen fuoz   unt was der vile grôz:
> dâ mite liuf er sô balde   sam daz tier dâ ze walde.
>
> Etlichiu bar daz chint   daz mit allen vieren gie
> sam daz rint.
>
> Sumeliche flurn begarewe   ir scônen varwe:
> si wurten swarz unt egelîch . . .

The poet chooses to make no reference to learned annota-
tions such as those of Isidor, for instance to the names of
these monstrous peoples[49] or to the regions which they
inhabit. The most likely explanation for this omission is
literary economy: however, while there is clear evidence
that written sources were used here, it is advisable to bear
in mind that from the ninth century onwards there
existed manuscripts of Hraban's *De Universo* containing
illustrations probably drawn from manuscripts of Isidore.
The fabulous peoples, moreover, were frequently
depicted in Cluniac churches and on medieval *Mappae
Mundi*;[50] we shall come later to illustrations of the
Alexander legend.[51] Even with the scholarly author of the
Wiener Genesis the possibility of such influences cannot
be disregarded.

Structurally, the description of outlandish peoples in this work is introduced (645) and concluded (658) by a mention of the Devil. With a reference to Seth, whose offspring are the children of God, as opposed to the descendants of Cain, who are the children of Belial, the *Wiener Genesis* then moves without further transition to the brief episode in which 'sconiu wîb' are born of Cain's line ('swie ubel si wâren   sô was in doch got gnâdich'), and the sons of Seth fall in love with them:

677 Dô dei gotes chint gesâhen   des tieveles chint
          sô wolgetâne,
      zesamene si gehîten,   micheliu chint gewunnen,
      gîgante die mâren,   allez ubel begunden si mêren.

Here we are on orthodox exegetical ground. (The Vulgate itself does not explicitly link the giants with the 'potentes a sæculo viri famosi' of Gen. vi. 4 and with the daughters of men, nor the latter with Cain.) A corresponding treatment is to be found in Anglo-Saxon and in the Old Saxon *Genesis*:[52]

119 Thann quâmun eft fan Kaina   kraftaga liudi,
      heliđos hardmuoda,   habdun im hugi strangan,
      uurêđan uuillean,   ni uueldun uualdandas
      lêra lêstian,   ac habdun im lêđan strîd;
      uuuohsun im uurisilîco: that uuas thiu *uuirsa*
          giburd,
      kuman fan Kaina.

Women from this line corrupt the retinue of Seth: from their union stem 'manno barn' hostile to God.

Rudolf von Ems reports in very similar terms in his *Weltchronik*, 645 ff. In doing so he passes over a detail (originating from Josephus) in his principal source, Peter Comestor's *Historia Scholastica*, Liber Genesis, xxxi: 'Nam multi angeli Dei, id est filii Seth, id est qui supra *filii Dei*, cum mulieribus coeuntes injuriosos filios genuerunt' (PL 198, 1081C). With this harmonizing formulation Comestor has drawn the sting from a controversy which aroused passionate emotions among the Early Fathers, and which can be traced back to the Greek text of Gen. VI. 1–4 in the Septuagint version. According to one reading, the 'sons of God', namely, are called there the ἄγγελοι τοῦ θεοῦ. From this arises the myth, narrated in detail in the apocryphal (First) Book of Enoch, 6.1 ff. (Charles, II, 191 ff.), that certain angels, the children of heaven, were seized by a reprehensible longing for the beautiful daughters of men. Two hundred of the angels descended to the earth and united with these women, engendering giants.[53] According to the Book of Jubilees 4.15 (Charles, II, 18 f.) the angels of the Lord descended in order 'that they should instruct the children of men, and that they should do judgement and uprightness on the earth'; they are thus dignified with the name of 'Watchers' or 'Watchers of the Earth', in accordance with Daniel IV. 10 ff. In this version too (4.22) they succumb to the charms of the daughters of men — according to one notably misogynist source the angels are actually seduced by the women (The Testament of Reuben 5,6 in Charles, II, 299; cf. 1 En. 6.1 and 8.1–2). In 2 Enoch some of the Watchers appear to have supported the rebellion of Satan, while another faction was smitten by desire and descended for this reason (Charles, II, 439 f., etc.). In punishment they now languish in a subterranean place of suffering, while the souls of their offspring (physically exterminated by the Flood) have become demons tempting mankind.[54] In Lactantius, *Divinae Institutiones*, II, 'De origine erroris', we read somewhat divergently: 'providens Deus . . . misit angelos ad tutelam cultumque generis humani . . . (They consorted with women) . . . Tum in cœlum ob peccata, quibus se immerserant, non recepti, ceciderunt in terram. Sic eos diabolus ex angelis Dei suos fecit satellites, ac ministros. (Their children become terrestrial demons.)'[55]

Here we are clearly in a region which promises some enlightenment on the subject of Wolfram's neutral angels who (471.20 f.) 'muosen ûf die erden / zuo dem selben steine'. Again, we can only note this in passing.[56]

The Vetus Latina, version E (= European text, edited by B. Fischer, 2, Genesis (Freiburg, 1951-4), p. 102) reads 'angeli dei'. The Vulgate replaces this by 'filii dei'; these, as we already established, come to be identified with the sons of Seth, while the 'filiæ hominum' are interpreted as the daughters of Cain. Among the Early Fathers of the Church, for instance Tertullian, 1 Enoch was still regarded as canonical, while Origenes, Jerome and Augustine already rejected it as apocryphal.[57] The polemics associated with this question, however, served to propagate a knowledge of its contents, and those elements important to us were known in the West. A key witness is Isidor, *Etym.*, XI, iii, 14: 'Falso autem opinantur quidam inperiti de Scripturis sanctis praevaricatores angelos cum filiabus hominum ante diluvium concubuisse, et exinde natos Gigantes, id est nimium grandes et fortes viros, de quibus terra conpleta est. Cynocephali appellantur eo quod canina capita habeant . . .'.[58] Isidor had named the Giants, Cynocephali and Cyclops together as 'monstra . . . gentium' a few lines earlier. Through such juxtapositions the impression gained currency that giants were not the only fruit of union with the angels.[59] The *Sex Aetates Mundi*, an Irish text of which manuscripts from the eleventh and succeeding centuries exist, reports that Seth's posterity begot children with the progeny of Cain and that 'thence sprung the monstrous creatures (*torothair*) of the world, giants (*fomoraig*) and leprechauns (*luchorpáin* — elves) and every monstrous illshapen form that people have had'.[60] These perished in the Flood, however. To counter this difficulty the text later repeats its assertion, this time applied to Cham, the spiritual heir of Cain, after the deluge: 'from him sprung leprechauns and giants and horseheads (*goborchind*), and every unshapely form besides that people have'.[61] James Carney assigns priority to the first of these two versions, assuming that this Irish tradition is dependent on Isidor and that it was known to the author of *Beowulf*.[62] Once more we are thus encouraged to consider the possibility of Irish mediation. It has, of course, long been recognized by Beowulf research — for the text clearly states the fact — that Grendel and his mother are progeny of Cain.[63] After the latter was condemned by the Creator he was banished, according to tradition, to a desolate land inhabited only by wild beasts. From Cain stemmed all evil, misshapen creatures: ogres, goblins and evil demons:[64] 111 ff. 'þanon untȳdras   ealle onwōcon, / eotenas ond ylfe   ond orcnêâs', not to mention the giants which defied God: 'swylce gīgantas,   þā wið Gode wunnon'.[65] Grendel's mother is portrayed as one such monster (1258 ff.), descended from Cain, who was forced to live in the 'icy currents of abominable lakes'. According to Jordanes — in a further ramification of this tradition — certain witches (*Haliurunnae*) were driven out by the Gothic leader Filimer; they consorted with evil spirits in the Scythian wilderness and bore by them the Huns.[66] The evidence quoted will suffice to show that the *Wiener Genesis* is by no means alone when it asserts that both the monstrous peoples and the giants are descendants of Cain, although the poet does not confuse their origin. How such traditions can coalesce is well illustrated by the Brandan legend[67] where Brandan encounters a fabulous people 'kegen das ôsterende' (1095) in paradise-like surroundings:

> 1249   ir houbte wâren als der swîn,
>   ir hende berîn und vûze hundîn,
>   cranches helse, menschlîche brust.

They prove to be neutral angels (1313 *der verstalte geist*). Reference is made to the fall of Lucifer, but not to Cain.

Thus armed we return to Wolfram: Monstrous beings from the East are vital to the very fabric of *Parzival*, since Wolfram assigns to one of them[68] — Cundrîe — a role of unique importance. It may be helpful to recapitulate some well-known facts about her physical appearance. Chrétien's *Roman de Perceval*[69] contains two parallel, but independent descriptions of ugly persons, the 'damoisele' (4611), who corresponds to Cundrîe[70] in *Parzival*, and the 'escuier desavenant' (6986) whom Gavains encounters. In *Parzival* the squire and Cundrîe are brother and sister, so that Wolfram is able to apply one basic description to both (313.1 ff. and 517.16 ff.). Wolfram accepts some features of Chrétien's ugly maiden, but disregards others,[71] such as the tiny, deep-set, rodent eyes, the bovine or asinine lips, the goat-like beard, twisted spine, hunched back and humped chest. More significant still, he has replaced these 'domestic' and agricultural analogies with others. By endowing them with dog-like muzzles, shaggy faces, boar's tusks, bristling hair (but cf. *Roman de Perceval*, 6989 f.), bears' ears, claws like those of a lion and ape-like skin, Wolfram has transformed Cundrîe and her brother into fabulous creatures which owe something to Chrétien and something to his own invention, but which in the combination of their most striking features have an unmistakable resemblance to the dog-

heads (Cynocephali)[72] and to other marvellous peoples of
the East. The so-called *Letter of Pharasmanes King of
Iberia to the Emperor Hadrian* about the marvels of Asia[73]
(Redaction D, xiv), reports of Cynocephali which possess
'aprorum dentes, canina capita, ignem et flammam
flantes' (it is diverting to ponder the appropriateness of
the latter remark to Wolfram's 'fire-breathing' Cundrîe!).
Elsewhere we read: 'Et aliae sunt mulieres ibi, dentes
aprorum habentes, capillos usque ad talos' (xxii). *The
Letter of Pharasmanes* contributed possibly to Isidor's
Etymologies, and certainly to the legend of Prester John
and, more influentially still, to the interpolated versions
of the *Historia de preliis*.[74] Thus the widely known redaction I² relates how Alexander the Great discovers giant
women 'dentes habentes aprorum et capillos usque ad
talos, reliquum corpus pilosum quasi strutio'.[75] Women
of this type are depicted in illuminated manuscripts of
not later than the end of the tenth century, in company
with animal- (more specifically lion-) headed and bristly-
backed monsters or giants from the *Letter of Pharasmanes*
tradition.[76] Already in Pliny's *Natural History* (vii, 2, 23)
the Cynocephali are said to be 'unguibus armatum', a
detail echoed by *Lucidarius*: 'in ist daz houbet gescaffen
nach den hunden, den die clawen sint groz unde crunb.
die vassint sich mit den ruhen húten die sie den tieren abe
ge ciehent . . . daz heizen wir hunt hóbete' (11, 28 ff.).[77]
An illustration in a manuscript of the late fourteenth
century (Munich, c.g.m. 7377) shows Alexander fighting
a group of Cynocephali with griffins' claws: this derives
from Ulrich von Etzenbach's *Alexander*, 23088 'und füeze
als der grîfen clân'.[78] It is easy to see how Wolfram —
although he was presumably exposed to a variety of
sources — could have drawn all the elements he needed
for the composite depiction of Cundrîe and her brother

from illustrated works relating to the exploits of Alexander in the fabulous East.[79] Indeed one may go further and assert that such matter, text and illumination, had a pronounced influence on western notions of exotic beings altogether.[80]

Before continuing, we must consider briefly the possible argument that Wolfram, in describing the Grail messenger, had in mind not only Chrétien's *Roman de Perceval* but also the monstrous 'vilain' encountered by Calogrenanz in a forest clearing (Yvain, 288 ff., cf. Hartmann, *Iwein*, 418 ff.; 526 'der ungehiure').[81] The 'vilain' does indeed have boar's tusks — 'danz de sangler' (304; Hartmann, 455 ff.), but he lacks those other original features of Wolfram's account which have occupied us, and in particular the combination of them. To put the description of Chrétien's 'vilain' and Hartmann's 'gebûre' in an adequate perspective would demand a comparative treatment of greater depth and extent than can be undertaken here;[82] this perspective I hope to supply elsewhere. For the moment we may note that the 'vilain' — like the ugly maiden in *Peredur* — can solve but few of the problems posed by Wolfram's description and that side by side with the rural elements of his physiognomy he himself possesses features clearly derived from the fabulous peoples of the East:[83] his boar's tusks, his wolf-like mouth, his great, elephantine ears, and, not least, his huge size and blackamoor-like appearance.[84] The equivalent figure in the Welsh romance *Iarlles y Ffynnawn* (*The Lady of the Fountain*) is a giant black Cyclops with one big foot.[85] Decisively, moreover, Wolfram's Cundrîe and her kin stem, quite explicitly, not from the Celtic forests, but from that very region of the East in which ancient natural historians and the Alexander legend locate the exotic races.

The *Liber Monstrorum*, which again belongs to the *Letter of Pharasmanes* tradition, identifies India as a prime region of monsters: 'Fluvius Indiae Ganges, qui aurum eum lapidibus profert pretiosis, mira monstruosae feritatis genera gignit'.[86] In Wolfram, Cundrîe and her brother stem from precisely this area ('bî dem wazzer Ganjas / ime lant ze Trîbalibôt', i.e. India).[87] Twice it is stressed that they are not individual monstrosities, but representatives of a separate and ancient people (517.30 and 519.5 ff.):

(Secundille)[88]   diu het in ir rîche
hart unlougenlîche
von alter dar der liute vil
mit verkêrtem antlützes zil:
si truogen vremdiu wilden mâl.

Wolfram, of course, does not release this information at the first appearance of Cundrîe, but reserves it, in his usual wilful fashion, for the description of her brother who is 'unglîch menschen bilde' (517. 24). In the overall context of this paper it is but a small step to conclude that Cundrîe and Malcrêatiure — this name, introduced by Wolfram, is highly significant — are not simply progeny of Adam, but more specifically *children of Cain*, like the corresponding creatures in the *Wiener Genesis*.[89] One may note here that the Middle English *Ywain and Gawain* follows Chrétien's depiction of the 'vilain' closely, but designates him explicitly as a 'karl of Kaymes kyn'.[90] Wolfram's cautious formulation certainly does not exclude this same interpretation. Adam's warning against specific herbs is no formality: the *êre* of the human race, and the *sælekeit* of those concerned is at stake (518.20 ff.). We are, no doubt deliberately, left in the dark as to which women disregarded this solemn warning:

518.25   diu wîp tâten et als wîp: (i.e. like Eve)
etslîcher (my italics) riet ir brœder lîp
daz si diu werc volbrâhte,
des ir herzen gir gedâhte.
sus wart verkêrt diu mennischeit . . .

The subject of Cain himself is introduced with similar
indefiniteness by Trevrizent (463.23 ff.). Adam and Eve
begot children — 'einem riet sîn ungenuht (precisely
the word used in Adam's warnings to his daughters in
518.14) / daz er durch gîteclîchen ruom (cf. the 'herzen
gir' of 518.28) / sîner anen nam den magetuom'. Not
until twenty lines later is Cain's name mentioned.

Let us now consider this problem from a different
viewpoint. Significantly, various accomplishments had
been attributed to Cundrîe even before the detailed
description of her appearance. She has a command of all
languages. In addition she is skilled in Dialectic, Geo-
metry, Astronomy, and Rhetoric (312.20 ff.).[91] The Grail
circle is not alone in depending on her pharmaceutical
experience. Gâwân is healed by Arnîve with salves and
herbs:

579.23   si sprach 'ich senfte iu schiere.
Cundrîe la surziere
ruochet mich sô dicke sehn:
swaz von erzenîe mac geschehn,
des tuot si mich gewaltec wol.
sît Anfortas in jâmers dol
kom, daz man im helfe warp,
diu salbe im half, daz er niht starp:
Si ist von Munsalvæsche komn.'

One may also reflect on how herbs for the treatment of
Anfortas were sought from the four rivers of Paradise
(481.19 ff.) if Cundrîe did not play at least an organizatory
role in their acquisition. Anfortas, after all, was suffering

from a poisoned wound inflicted by a heathen from
Ethnîse, 'dâ ûzzem pardîse / rinnet diu Tigris'
(479.15 ff.). Recourse to Cundrîe is thus quite natural.
Anfortas's sick-room (789.21 ff.) is full of products of the
East:[92] the floor is strewn with fragrant herbs and
spices, many of which have paradisaic associations, his
bed is braced with fire-resistant 'strangen von sala-
mander', and a whole section, notoriously, is devoted to
the jewels of the bed:

> 792.2   ze sælde unt ze erzenîe guot,
> was dâ maneges steines sunder art.
> vil kraft man an in innen wart,
> derz versuochen kund mit listen.[93]

Who has such knowledge more abundantly than Cundrîe?
The oriental origin of most precious stones is taken for
granted, not only in sources like the *Etymologies*, but in all
reports of marvels.[94] In the very passage which describes
the nature of Cundrîe and Malcrêatiure we learn that
Queen Secundille was astonished that the wealth of the
Grail king can be said to excel her own 'wan vil wazzer
(i.e. the rivers of Paradise) in ir lant truoc / für den griez
edel gesteine' (519.10 ff.). Accordingly, when Cundrîe
and her brother are sent as gifts to Anfortas they bring
with them priceless treasures. Astronomical insights,
again, play an important role in the medical treatment
of Anfortas, as in the work at large;[95] once more the
central importance of Cundrîe becomes apparent. To
prevent his audience from regarding these skills as merely
her personal possession, Wolfram describes Malcrêatiure
too as 'der würze unt der sterne mâc' — making it clear
that this is no casual or individual affinity.[96]

What is the origin of these skills and this knowledge,
for which the Christian Grail is dependent upon the

heathen East? According to 518.1 ff. we might assume
that this lore is simply inherited from Adam. This view is
not wholly satisfactory, however, above all because it
does not explain — or does so purely on the basis of
mere proximity to the earthly Paradise — why key aspects
of this knowledge are restricted to a small and — at first
sight dubious and unworthy — segment of humanity in
the Orient. In addition Cundrîe is known as 'la surziere',
although her powers are clearly interpreted as 'white
magic', the word 'nigrômanzî' being applied in *Parzival*
only to Clinschor.[97] Now the children of Cain are known
according to Genesis iv. 19 ff. as the inaugurators of
various arts: they are skilful with musical instruments,[98]
at the forge, and in the hunt, compare Rudolf von Ems,
Weltchronik, 520 ff. The *Wiener Genesis* as we saw earlier,
has Cain teach his children 'dei zouber dei hiute sint'
(643). But where can one find evidence which compre-
hends not only most aspects of Cundrîe's knowledge, but
also the superb workmanship in precious stones and
metals which so astonishes the Arthurian circle when
they inspect the armour of Feirefîz, and which makes it
possible to interpret all these skills as the peculiar possession of a monstrous people and of those among whom they
live in the neighbourhood of Paradise?[99] The answer, once
more, is to be found in the First Book of Enoch: [The
Angels, the Watchers] took unto themselves wives . . .
and they taught them charms and enchantments, and
the cutting of roots, and made them acquainted with
plants. And they became pregnant, and they bare great
giants . . . And Azâzêl [their leader] taught men to make
swords, and knives, and shields, and breastplates, and
made known to them the metals [of the earth] and the
art of working them, and bracelets, and ornaments, and
the use of antimony, and the beautifying of the eyelids,

3

and all kinds of costly stones, and all colouring tinctures (7.1 ff.; Charles, II, 192). Other angels taught the daughters of Cain astrology, knowledge of the constellations, of the clouds, the signs of the earth, the signs of the sun, and the course of the moon. This passage[100] is known to the Early Fathers of the Church, for instance Tertullian, who reproduces it in detail,[101] and like other authors, uses it as a starting point for strictures on women which bear more than a passing resemblance to certain formulations in *Parzival* (above all in the Prologue 2.23 ff., compare 116.5 ff. — to be seen together with criticisms of cosmetics, see 551.27 ff. and 776.8 ff.; one may refer here, also, to the fashionable elegance of Cundrîe, which may serve not merely as a contrast to her looks, but could be a further pointer to her origin). [102] It is probably idle to speculate about the exact sources (or informants?) through which Wolfram may have acquired this knowledge,[103] but we are at least on firmer ground to the extent that we can take for granted his acquaintance with the related tradition of the neutral angels — and even with their role as 'Watchers' (here as the original custodians of the Grail).

In exploring Wolfram's possible motives in not designating Cundrîe and Malcrêatiure unambiguously as children of Cain one might point first of all to his well-known penchant for obscurantism. At the same time it must be remembered that the Cainites were a heretical sect much condemned in the late twelfth century — Wolfram would hardly have wished this particular association to suggest itself to his hearers. It may be, moreover, that the outward appearance of the Grail Messenger and her brother, together with the latter's name Malcrêatiure, were of themselves commentary enough for a medieval audience, who might very well have placed a highly negative interpretation on Cundrîe's physiognomy, had not Wolfram forestalled and counter-balanced this by his reference to her 'triwen wol gelobt' and to her striking accomplishments (312.2; 312.19 ff.).[104] The Evangelists, admittedly, are occasionally depicted as animal-headed,[105] while St Christopher himself is portrayed in the earlier versions of his *Passio* as a man-eating dog-head, who was converted to Christianity and martyred.[106] The alarm the appearance of this saint evokes in his persecutors, however, only confirms the understandably cautious reaction to Cynocephali in general. The *Revelations* of Pseudo-Methodius, one of the most popular books of the Middle Ages, includes them ('Anuphagii [i.e. Anthropophagi] qui dicuntur Cyno-cephali') among the unclean peoples who were enclosed by Alexander the Great, and who will break out in the Last Days, wreaking destruction on the earth.[107] Of these peoples, which are sometimes deemed to include the Huns, the Alans and the Goths, the Hereford map (late thirteenth century) notes: 'Hic sunt homines trucu-lenti nimis, humanis carnibus vescentes, cruorem potantes, *filii Caini maledicti*' (my italics).[108] The boar's tusks, bristles, shaggy face, bear's ears and ape-like skin of Cundrîe could likewise have suggested an association with sin, the devil or even the Antichrist,[109] while her 'pfæwîn huot' (313.10, cf. 225.12) also lends itself to spiritual interpretation. Yet Wolfram spurns the oppor-tunity for explicitness offered by Chrétien's comment that never did anything so ugly exist even in hell (*Roman de Perceval*, 4618 f.). At the same time, Wolfram specifies the historical descent and geographical provenance of Cundrîe, yet avoids identifying her irrevocably with any specific monstrous race, making her into a composite[110] and, by this means also, essentially ambivalent figure.

In the last instance, the reason for Wolfram's reticence here may be sought not simply in narrative predilection or in incorrigible personal bent, but in his wish to allow the outwardly disordered, yet at heart loyal and helpful figure of Cundrîe — standing, in a way that challenges his audience's prejudices, for the ostensibly least attractive elements of the heathen world, the 'filii Caini maledicti' — to play a benevolent and in no way demonic role in a process of world-wide reconciliation. Under Parzival, as Grail King, with Cundrîe bearing the Grail emblem of the turtle dove (783.23), and with Repanse de schoye replacing the dead Secundille as wife of Feirefîz, queen of India (822.20 ff.), the children of Adam are symbolically reunited. Christian rule now extends to the very borders of Paradise, which itself remains for ever physically inaccessible.

Wolfram, I suggest moreover, could hardly overlook the poetic force of a situation in which Parzival, who himself shares the stigma of the first murderer (464.16 ff.) following his killing of Ithêr, is denounced in front of the whole Round Table by a descendant of Cain, and then, like Cain himself, becomes 'fluhtiger unt wadalêre ze vile manegeme jâre' (WG, 641). After Cundrîe's explicit reference to Ithêr (315.11–12), what irony speaks from her words to Parzival, whose inner *disordinatio*, she believes, corresponds to the outward corruption of the image of God which she has inherited from Cain or his progeny:

> 315.24   ich dunke iuch ungehiure,
> und bin gehiurer doch dann ir

— in what is one of the great moments of the work. How appropriate, then, that Cundrîe in Book xv, after naming the seven planets, as a sign that the hero will

enter into the sovereignty once enjoyed by Adam
(782.18 ff.),[111] now dissociates Parzival from that *ungenuht*[112] which led to the sin of Cain,[113] to that of his
daughters, and, as she had earlier assumed, to Parzival's
own murderous act, an *ungenuht* externalized in the
hideous appearance of both herself and Malcrêatiure
(520.1 f. Von wîbes gir ein underscheit / in schiet von
der mennescheit). Now, Trevrizent, without any risk of
bringing Parzival to despair, can also reveal the truth
about the fate of the 'vertriben geiste', once custodians
of the Grail. As, once again, the Books of Enoch and the
Book of Jubilees repeatedly affirm:[114]

> 798.16   got ist stæt mit sölhen siten,
>   er strîtet iemmer wider sie . . .
>   êweclîch sint si verlorn.

REFERENCES

[1] This paper was first delivered, in German, at the third Anglo-German
Colloquium in Cambridge (September 1971) and subsequently in English, at the
Institute of Germanic Studies, University of London (May 1972). In writing and
in revising it I have profited from suggestions by colleagues and friends, in
particular by Ursula and Peter Dronke, Christoph Gerhardt, Wolfgang Harms,
Peter Hurst, Partha Mitter, and Friedrich Ohly. Any errors are my own.

[2] Kathryn Smits, *Die frühmittelhochdeutsche 'Wiener Genesis'. Kritische Ausgabe
mit einem einleitenden Kommentar zur Überlieferung*, Philologische Studien und
Quellen, 59 (Berlin, 1972).

[3] See, for example, Paul Hagen, *Der Gral*, Quellen und Forschungen, 85
(Straßburg, 1900), p. 16; Samuel Singer, 'Zu Wolframs *Parzival*' in *Abhandlungen
zur germanischen Philologie. Festgabe für Richard Heinzel* (Halle a.S., 1898), pp. 406 f.
Barbara Seitz, *Die Darstellung häßlicher Menschen in mittelhochdeutscher erzählender
Literatur von der 'Wiener Genesis' bis zum Ausgang des 13. Jahrhunderts* (Inaugural-
Dissertation Tübingen, 1967), p. 63, explains the origin of the myth as arising
from Augustine's views on the possible descent of the exotic peoples from
Adam, combined with the notion that India, their homeland, was also considered
the site of the earthly paradise. This explanation cannot be ruled out, but it
is unsatisfactory on several scores, not least because it does not account for the
kernel of the story (the daughters of Adam, and Adam's warning against the
noxious herbs).

[4] Pliny, *Natural History*, VII, Books XXIV–XXVII, edited and translated by
W. H. S. Jones, The Loeb Classical Library (London and Cambridge, Massachusetts, 1966) contains a wealth of examples, many of them relevant in our
context; see, *inter alia*, XXV, 5, 15 ('inde et plerosque ita video existimare nihil
non herbarum vi effici posse'); XXIV, 92, 143; XXVI, 90, 151–62. See also *Hand-*

wörterbuch des deutschen Aberglaubens, VI, 1713 ff.; IX, 448 and A. Weller, *Die frühmittelhochdeutsche 'Wiener Genesis'*, Palaestra, 123 (Berlin, 1914), p. 192, O. F. Emerson, *PMLA*, 21 (1906), 884, and Hugo Kuhn, *Dichtung und Welt im Mittelalter* (Stuttgart, 1959), p. 159. Thomas of Cantimpré, *De naturis rerum*, reprint of prologue in *Vivarium*, 5 (1967), p. 154, accounts for discrepancies in his authorities by postulating differing 'naturas et mores animalium aut effectus herbarum' in West and East. The existence of forbidden and magic herbs constitutes an international folklore motif.

⁵ Fr. Wilhelm, *Denkmäler deutscher Prosa des 11. und 12. Jahrhunderts* (Munich, 1960), A, pp. 42 ff. and B, pp. 88 ff. The Latin heading is derived from the later Cod. Vindob. 1118, fol. 79v, see Wilhelm, B, p. 101. Cf. also Gustav Ehrismann, *Geschichte der deutschen Literatur*, II, 1, p. 234.

⁶ Pliny ascribes this latter effect to the *dracunculus*, *Nat. Hist.*, XXIV, 92, 143. One may also recall here the properties of the mandrake root. The chaste elephant, typologically linked to Adam and Eve, is said to procure this in Paradise, or 'in proximum paradysi'; it ensures the conception of its young (*Der ... Physiologus* in Wilhelm, *Denkmäler*, A, p. 15, cf. B, p. 26). The mandrake also plays a role in the *Wiener Genesis* (1357=Gen. xxx. 16). For literature on the mandrake, see *Handwb.d.dt.Aberglaubens*, I, 311 ff. Cf. also the *Midrash Rabbah*, Genesis, I, translated by H. Freedman (London, 1939), p. 194: 'The men of the generation of the Flood ... each took two wives, one for procreation and the other for sexual gratification. The former would stay like a widow throughout her life, while the latter was given to drink a potion of roots, so that she should not bear.' Cf. Fr. Zarncke, *Der Priester Johannes*, I, *Abh.d.philol.-hist. Cl. d. Kgl. Sächs. Ges. d. Wiss. zu Leipzig*, 7 (1879), 912: an Indian preparation made in part of 'salutiferis herbis ... valet non valentibus generare, etiam mulieribus non valentibus concipere'.

⁷ See P. W. Hurst, 'The Theme of the Earthly Paradise and Associated Traditions in Middle High German Literature, with Particular Reference to the *Wiener Genesis* and the *Tristan* of Gottfried von Straßburg' (unpublished Ph.D. dissertation, University of Cambridge, in preparation) with full references to exegetical and secondary literature. According to Alcuin, *Interrogationes et responsiones in Genesin*, the tree of life served 'quasi medicina', the tree of knowledge 'quasi ut veneno' (PL 100, 517D–518A). The same source states that poisonous herbs did not exist until after the Fall (PL 100, 524D).

⁸ A twelfth-century example of this view is to be found in Petrus Comestor, *Historia Scholastica* (Liber Genesis, XXVIII. PL 198, 1079C): 'quia non erat usus carnium ante diluvium'. Cf. *The Babylonian Talmud, Sanhedrin*, I, translated by H. Freedman (London, 1935), p. 404: 'Adam was not permitted to eat flesh ... But with the advent of the sons of Noah, it was permitted.' See also Louis Ginzberg, *The Legends of the Jews*, translated from the German manuscript by Henrietta Szold, 7 vols (Philadelphia, 1913–38), I, 71.

⁹ See Ernst Martin, Commentary on *Parzival*, 518.1 ff. and 518.15 ff. (Halle a.S., 1903). Reference is also made here to *Reinfrid von Braunschweig* (cf. Singer, 'Zu Wolframs *Parzival*', p. 466).

¹⁰ Karl Schorbach, *Studien über das deutsche Volksbuch 'Lucidarius' und seine Bearbeitungen in fremden Sprachen*, Quellen und Forschungen, 74 (Straßburg, 1894), p. 193 and pp. 227 f. See also Weller, *Die frühmittelhochdeutsche 'Wiener Genesis'*, e.g. pp. 71 f.

¹¹ Julius Schwietering, 'Natur und *art*'. In *Philologische Schriften*, edited by Friedrich Ohly and Max Wehrli (Munich, 1969), considers these lines with reference to certain aspects of Genesis commentary (pp. 457 f.) and later interprets *Parzival*, 518.18 ff. (pp. 466 f. and p. 471).

¹² *The Vorau 'Moses' and 'Balaam'. A Study of their Relationship to Exegetical Tradition*, MHRA Dissertation Series, 2 (Cambridge, 1970), pp. 148 f.

[13] The notion of 'celestial man' was employed by the *Zohar*. In its forerunner, the *Bahir* ('Radiance'), which was composed in twelfth-century Provence, Primordial Man combines in himself the ten Sefiroth (emanations of the primal light — the first corresponding to the head) and thus reflects the structure of the cosmos, see B. J. Bamberger, *Fallen Angels* (Philadelphia, 1952), pp. 168 ff. This idea appears to go back to early gnostic forms of speculation, cf. *The Encyclopaedia of the Jewish Religion*, edited by R. J. Zwi Werblowsky and G. Wigoder (Jerusalem-Tel Aviv, 1966), p. 12, and W. Bousset, *Hauptprobleme der Gnosis* (Göttingen, 1907), pp. 171 ff.

[14] On the size and physical perfection of Adam before the Fall, see Ginzberg, I, 59 and v, 79. According to *The Babylonian Talmud, Sanhedrin*, 11, p. 678, the height of Adam was 100 cubits; his two heels appear to the observer like two orbs of the sun, *The Babylonian Talmud, Baba Bathra*, 1, translated by M. Simon (London, 1935), p. 233. A. H. Krappe, 'Bene Elohim', *Studi e Materiali di Storia delle Religioni*, 9 (1933), 158: Adam is a giant in Rabbinic and Mohammedan traditions, while Irish and ancient Scandinavian sources consider the first inhabitants of the earth to have been giants. Ute Schwab, 'Zur zweiten Fitte des *Heliand*', *Mediaevalia Litteraria*, Festschrift für Helmut de Boor, edited by Ursula Hennig and Herbert Kolb (Munich, 1971), p. 93, speaks of the 'engelsgleich strahlende Urvollkommenheit Adams in der gottebenbildlichen Schönheit, dem Lichtleib des verklärten Menschen'; see too R. Scroggs, *The Last Adam. A Study in Pauline Anthropology* (Oxford, 1966), p. 24: 'Adam is God's perfect man . . . created with a nature of plenitude and power' and A. M. Haas, 'Der Lichtsprung der Gottheit (*Parz.* 466)', *FS M. Wehrli* (Zürich, 1969), pp. 219 ff., notes 64–71, both cited by Schwab. For early Welsh references to the beauty, wisdom and might of Adam, see *Trioedd Ynys Prydein. The Welsh Triads*, edited and translated by R. Bromwich (Cardiff, 1961), pp. 122–8.

[15] Only a few characteristic examples can be cited here: John Chrysostom, *Homiliæ in Genesim*, PG 53, 116, 5: 'cogita quantæ fuerit sapientiæ tot generibus . . . propria et convenientia suæ naturæ imponere nomina'; Angelom of Luxeuil, *Commentarius in Genesin*, PL 115, 134B: 'Hic enim juxta litteram ostenditur quanta dignitate homo pecoribus et animalibus irrationabilibus antecellit, qui intellectu suo cuncta distinguere et nominatim discernere potuit, et secundum qualitates, mores et iras bestiarum nomina imposuit.' Of Jewish sources, see for example *Midrash Rabbah*, Numbers, 11, translated by J. J. Slotki (London, 1939), p. 750: '[The ministering angels said to the Holy One]: "What is man, that Thou art mindful of him" (Ps. VIII. 5). He answered them: "The man whom I desire to create will possess wisdom that shall exceed yours." ' In *Midrash Rabbah*, Ecclesiastes, translated by A. Cohen (London, 1939), p. 204, the angels were at a loss when asked to name the animals, but Adam succeeded in doing so. Cf. Ginzberg, I, 61 and v, 83, particularly with reference to Adam's prophetic gift.

[16] For instance *The Babylonian Talmud, Sanhedrin*, 1, translated by J. Shachter, p. 241: 'The dust of the first man was gathered from all parts of the earth'; cf. Ginzberg, *Legends*, I, 54 f. and v, 72 f. Also of interest in this context is the notion that the name Adam signifies 'red', since he was formed of the virgin soil of earth (Hebrew âdôm 'red'; adâmah 'ground'), cf. Josephus, *Antiquities*, I, 34; a typical, if derivative medieval example: Angelom of Luxeuil, *Comm. in Gen.*: 'Adam interpretatur *homo*, sive *terrenus*, sive *terra rubra*' (PL 115, 134C). *Parzival* scholarship has drawn a parallel between this interpretation and Parzival's red armour, see W. J. Schröder, *Die Soltane-Erzählung in Wolframs 'Parzival'* (Heidelberg, 1963), pp. 73 ff. and note 25, with reference to P. Wapnewski.

[17] R. E. McNally, *The Bible in the Early Middle Ages*, Woodstock Papers, 4 (Maryland, 1959), pp. 26 f.

[18] In a paper delivered at the Oxford Patristics Conference, 1971 ('Early "Irish" Biblical Exegesis': the proceedings are to be published in the series *Texte und Untersuchungen zur Geschichte der altchristlichen Literatur*), Clare Stancliffe, while giving early Irish exegetes less credit for originality than do, e.g. B. Bischoff, and R. E. McNally, 'The Imagination and Early Irish Biblical Exegesis', *Annuale Medievale*, 10 (1969), 5–27, confirms their mediatory role and stresses that where, in Irish exegesis, 'we find apparently original interpretations or bizarre inventions these can generally be traced to the use of obscure sources, particularly apocrypha', which had a wide circulation in the Ireland of the time. Similar conclusions to the latter are reached by B. O. Murdoch, 'An Early Irish Adam and Eve: *Saltair na Rann* and the Traditions of the Fall' (to appear in Medieval Studies, 1973). I am grateful to both scholars for access to their typescripts.

[19] *The Apocrypha and Pseudepigrapha of the Old Testament in English*, edited by R. H. Charles, et al. (Oxford, 1913). Volume II, *Pseudepigrapha*, p. 449, with note 13 and the Introduction to 2 Enoch (pp. 425 ff.). A. Vaillant, *Le Livre des secrets d'Hénoch. Texte slave et traduction française* (Paris, 1952), has demonstrated — against Charles, et al. — the priority of the shorter version and has outlined the role of the principal reviser. Vaillant's views on the Jewish-Christian origin and the dating of the work have since been modified by Arie Rubinstein, 'Observations on the Slavonic book of Enoch', *The Journal of Jewish Studies*, 13 (1962), 1–21.

[20] See *Die religiösen Dichtungen des 11. und 12. Jahrhunderts*, edited by Fr. Maurer, 1 (Tübingen, 1964), p. 286 (Vorau *Ezzolied*) and p. 311 (*Summa Theologiae*), also the comments of H. Freytag, *Kommentar zur frühmittelhochdeutschen 'Summa Theologiae'*, Medium Aevum. Philologische Studien, 19 (Munich, 1970), pp. 74–82 and '*Summa Theologiae*', Strophe 9 und 10: Der Mensch als Mikrokosmos' (forthcoming: to appear in the proceedings of the Cambridge Anglo-German Colloquium, September 1971). For Wolfram see W. Deinert, *Ritter und Kosmos im 'Parzival'. Eine Untersuchung der Sternkunde Wolframs von Eschenbach*, Münchener Texte und Untersuchungen zur deutschen Literatur des Mittelalters, 2 (Munich, 1960), p. 108.

[21] J. M. Evans, 'Microcosmic Adam', *Medium Aevum*, 35 (1966), 38–42, concludes that, by whatever channels, this version of Adam's constitution 'seems to have been known in England before the end of the tenth century' (pp. 38 f.). Cf. McNally, *The Bible*, pp. 27 f.

[22] Quoted by L. Troje, 'ΑΔΑΜ und ΖΩΗ. Eine Szene der altchristlichen Kunst in ihrem religionsgeschichtlichen Zusammenhange', SB der Heidelberger Akad. d. Wiss., Phil-hist. Kl., 17 (Heidelberg, 1916), p. 21; pp. 13 ff., the genesis of the belief in Adam's splendour before the Fall.

[23] *Lexikon der christlichen Ikonographie*, 1 (Freiburg i. Br., 1968), p. 45.

[24] Compare for instance *Midrash Rabbah*, Genesis 1, p. 200, with *The Babylonian Talmud, Baba Mezi'a*, translated by H. Freedman (London, 1935), p. 493 (and note 4). Also Ginzberg, *Legends*, 1, 61; v, 82.

[25] This is the so-called Book of Raziel, cf. Ginzberg, *Legends*, 1, 91 ff., and v, 117 f.; also Wells, p. 149.

[26] J. Baltrušaitis, *Le Moyen Âge fantastique. Antiquités et exotismes dans l'art gothique* (Paris, 1955), p. 26.

[27] Adam's astronomical knowledge is widely attested. Cf. the section above on his cosmic affinities, and earlier *Parzival* literature, e.g. Hagen, *Der Gral*, pp. 19 f.; also *Handwörterbuch des deutschen Aberglaubens*, 1 (Berlin and Leipzig, 1927), 164. On Pythagoras in *Parzival* see Herbert Kolb, 'Isidorsche "Etymologien" im *Parzival*', in *Wolfram-Studien*, edited by Werner Schröder (Berlin, 1970), pp. 132 ff. Kolb's demonstration of Wolfram's indebtedness to the *Etymologies* — which could be amplified without difficulty — is of particular interest here in view of the prominence given to references from Isidor at key points of the

present article. See also *Herzog Ernst*, edited by K. Bartsch (Vienna, 1869),
pp. CLXVI–CLXXII: Isidor is seen as the immediate source of references to the
'kananäischen Riesen' (p. CLXXII) in the Ernst legend and in *Reinfrid*.

[28] Lexikon der christlichen Ikonographie, I, 46 f.

[29] Wells, p. 149.

[30] Charles, II, p. 126.

[31] Charles, II, pp. 138 (xxii, 1) and 148 (xxix, 1–2). Cf. the Book of Jubilees
3. 27 (Charles, II, 17).

[32] This prose 'Auflösung' is based on a verse redaction of which fourteenth-
century manuscripts exist, see *Ein deutsches Adambuch. Nach einer ungedruckten
Handschrift der Hamburger Stadtbibliothek aus dem XV. Jahrhundert*, edited by Hans
Vollmer (Progr. Hamburg, 1908), p. iii and pp. 46 ff. Moreover, allusions to
individual episodes of the *Vita* suggest that knowledge of it in Germany goes
back much further, cf. W. J. Schröder, *Die Soltane-Erzählung*, pp. 68 f. and
note 22. Murdoch, 'An early Irish Adam and Eve' shows that the author of the
Early Middle Irish *Saltair na Rann* (late tenth century) was acquainted with the
Vita, while Clare Stancliffe, 'Early "Irish" Biblical Exegesis', finds possible
evidence of its use in an early St Gall MS.

[33] Charles, II, 152. Seth is present with thirty brothers and thirty sisters.

[34] *The Latin Josephus*, edited by Franz Blatt, I, *Introduction and Text. The Antiquities*, Books I–V. Acta Jutlandica, 30, i (Copenhagen, 1958), p. 15. The relevant
passage reads: 'duas facientes columnas, aliam quidem ex lateribus, aliam vero ex
lapidibus' (p. 132, 14). Rudolf von Ems, *Weltchronik*, 682 ff., also derives the
episode from Josephus via Petrus Comestor's *Historia Scholastica*.

[35] St Bernard regards *curiositas* as the lowest step on the ladder of Pride (*De
gradibus humilitatis et superbiae*, PL 182, 958 ff.), see M. Schapiro, 'On the Aesthetic
Attitude in Romanesque Art', in *Art and Thought* (London, 1948), pp. 134 f.,
quoted by H. W. Janson, *Apes and Ape Lore in the Middle Ages and the Renaissance*,
Studies of the Warburg Institute, 20 (London, 1952), p. 112. On the vices of
Eve in the *Wiener Genesis* (e.g. 354) see B. Murdoch, *The Fall of Man in the Early
Middle High German Biblical Epic: The 'Wiener Genesis', the 'Vorauer Genesis' and the
'Anegenge'*, Göppinger Arbeiten zur Germanistik, 58 (Göppingen, 1972), pp.
77–80. This subject is discussed with insight already by San-Marte (A. Schulz),
'Parcival'-Studien, 2. Heft (Halle, 1861), pp. 85 ff.

[36] In Jubilees 10, 9 ff. (Charles, II, p. 28), Noah is taught by angels to combat
the diseases and seductions of the demons (descendants of the Watchers, see
below) with the herbs of the earth. His knowledge of medicine was written down
in a book, given eventually to his eldest son Shem, whose domain, Asia, includes
the Earthly Paradise, India, Ceylon and the homes of the monstrous peoples —
see e.g. Rudolf von Ems, *Weltchronik*, 1374 ff., and the later parts of this study.
A Latin version of the Jubilees dates from the mid-fifth century, but is only
fragmentarily preserved, see Charles, II, p. 3.

[37] Seitz, *Die Darstellung häßlicher Menschen*, p. 63 and note 81 (p. 85), observes
that according to Isidor *Etymologies*, XI, 4, some deformities, although not specifically those of the exotic peoples as she implies, are brought about 'sive magicis
cantibus, sive herbarum veneficio'. Isidor makes no reference in this context
to Adam or his daughters, however. It may be noted in passing that in *Ein
deutsches Adambuch*, p. 15, 16 ff., Eve ignorantly attributes the conception of her
first child (Cain) to 'ain arges krawt das ich in der wildnüs ass'. The child fetches
'gar ain süezz kraut aus dem wald' to reassure his mother.

[38] Janson, *Apes and Ape Lore*, pp. 94 f. and Montague R. James, *Description of
an Illuminated Manuscript of the Thirteenth Century in the Possession of Bernard Quaritch*
(London, 1904), pp. 15 f. The Latin quotations provided here are from the
latter.

[39] Karl Bartsch in his *Parzival* edition (note to 518.1) assumes 'eine talmudische Quelle' for the story. To my knowledge, this has never been corroborated.

[40] The *Canticles* version contains certain elements with no parallels in the relevant German sources, however, e.g. the reference to Damascus and to the plant-like souls of the offspring, as well as the comparison with Old Testament figures. For a (late) reference to Adam at Damascus see Jacob Grimm, 'Die Ungleichen Kinder Evas', *ZfdA*, 2 (1842), 263. Petrus Comestor, *Hist. Schol.*, reports that Adam was sent out of Paradise 'in agrum scilicet Damascenum, de quo sumptus fuerat, in quo Cain Abel suum fratrem interfecit (Gen. IV), juxta quem Adam, et Eva sepulti sunt in spelunca duplici' (PL 100, 1075B).

[41] Seitz, p. 63. It is also perhaps significant that a French ivory panel of the mid-ninth century depicts Adam and Eve under the Tree of Knowledge, surrounded by luxuriant vegetation. Depicted below them are animals, but also monsters, including centaurs, sirens, cynocephali, satyrs, a griffin, and a unicorn, cf. A Goldschmidt, *Die Elfenbeinskulpturen aus der Zeit der karolingischen und sächsischen Kaiser, VIII.–XI. Jahrhundert* (Berlin, 1914–18), I, no. 158 (p. 77) and Plate LXX. See also F. Klingender, *Animals in Art and Thought to the End of the Middle Ages*, London, 1971, page 170. Apulian portal and window-enclosures are frequently decorated with animals and monsters in plant-scrolls (ibid., p. 282).

[42] The starting point for any consideration of this topic must still be the admirable treatise by Oliver F. Emerson, 'Legends of Cain, Especially in Old and Middle English', *PMLA*, 21 (1906), 831–929, to which the present study is indebted at numerous points. Emerson's tribute to his own predecessors (p. 878, note 1) gives credit *inter alia* to Jacob Grimm, *Deutsche Mythologie* (1835, third edition 1854) for first calling attention to the Hebrew legend of Cain and his posterity, as explaining Grendel's descent from Cain in *Beowulf*.

[43] A survey of the evidence is provided by Emerson, pp. 832 ff.; Ginzberg, *Legends*, I, 105 and v, 133. Some Jewish sources report that Adam and Eve lived apart for 130 years after the Fall. During this time Adam fathered all the demons; their mothers included Lilith (who is elsewhere Adam's first wife), see Singer, 'Zu Wolframs *Parzival*', pp. 407 ff. According to another variant Adam and Eve both consorted with demons during their period of separation: male demons thus descend from Adam, female from Eve. See W. G. Soldan, *Geschichte der Hexenprozesse*, I, revised H. Heppe (Stuttgart, 1880), p. 175; also Ginzberg, *Legends*, I, 65; I, 113; v, 87. It seems reasonable to assume that the story of *Die Ungleichen Kinder Evas* is related to these traditions; in this context it is interesting to note the version ('Die Erschaffung der Unterirdischen') recorded by Karl Müllenhoff in *Sagen, Märchen und Lieder der Herzogthümer Schleswig Holstein und Lauenburg* (Kiel, 1845), p. 279 (no. 379). Cain is sometimes named as head of the 'ugly' faction, see Jacob Grimm, *ZfdA*, 2 (1842), 259 ff.

[44] See A. K. Stevens, 'Rudolf von Ems's *Barlaam und Josaphat*: Aspects of its Relationship to Christian Rhetorical Tradition, With a Consideration of its Thematic Structure' (unpublished Ph.D. dissertation, University of Cambridge, 1971), especially Chapter I.

[45] *Isidori Hispalensis Episcopi Etymologiarum Sive Originum, Libri XX*, edited by W. M. Lindsay, 2 vols, reprint (London, 1966). See Weller, *Die frühmittelhochdeutsche 'Wiener Genesis'*, pp. 53 f. and Seitz, *Die Darstellung häßlicher Menschen*, p. 69.

[46] Seitz, p. 64 and, in most particulars already, San-Marte, *'Parcival'-Studien*, II, p. 87 (not listed by Seitz).

[47] On the ancient and medieval traditions regarding these races see R. Wittkower, 'Marvels of the East. A Study in the History of Monsters', *Journal of the Warburg and Courtauld Institutes*, 5 (1942), 159–97. My distinction between malformed individuals and monstrous races goes back to Augustine, *De Civ. Dei*, XVI.8 (quoted by Wittkower, pp. 167 f. and Hagen, *Der Gral*, pp. 22–4) and beyond him to Pliny, *Nat. Hist.*, VII, 2, 32.

[48] See Lactantius, *Epitome divinarum institutionum*, cap. 25 (PL 6, 1032–3) for the etymology of ἄνθρωπος as 'he who looks upward (to God)'. Cited by Janson, *Apes*, p. 81 and note 31. Cf. the quotation from (Ps.) Bede in Schwietering, '*Natur und art*', p. 458.

[49] *Etym.*, XI, 3, 15 ff.: the corresponding Latin names in Isidor are Cynocephali, Blemmyae, Sciopodes, Artabatitae. The order of the two latter is reversed compared with Isidor, who mentions many more races. Weller, pp. 21 ff. refers to characteristic omissions by the poet.

[50] Wittkower, 'Marvels', pp. 174 ff., with references.

[51] Besides Wittkower see now D. J. A. Ross, *Illustrated Medieval Alexander-Books in Germany and the Netherlands. A Study in Comparative Iconography*, Publications of the MHRA, 3 (Cambridge, 1971).

[52] Edited by Otto Behaghel, *Heliand und Genesis*, sixth edition, Altdeutsche Textbibliothek, 4 (Halle (Saale), 1948); this passage is cited by Emerson, p. 891.

[53] See Ferdinand Dexinger, *Sturz der Göttersöhne oder Engel vor der Sintflut? Versuch eines Neuverständnisses von Genesis 6, 2–4*, Wiener Beiträge zur Theologie, 13 (Vienna, 1966). This work constitutes an excellent guide to the history of this crux, with bibliography, pp. 11–21 and a review of Jewish and Christian exegesis (pp. 88–124). The 'angel' interpretation of Gen. VI. 4, under the influence of the Book of Enoch, dominates Christian sources until the fourth century and is then replaced by the 'Sethite' interpretation. The latter is probably Syrian in origin but is first found in the work of Julius Africanus († c. 240), who had close connexions to the royal court of Edessa. No less useful, B. J. Bamberger, *Fallen Angels*; see also the lucid, if partially superseded account in Emerson, pp. 920–6.

[54] The origin of the demons is more frequently explained in this way than in that discussed above, p. 34, note 43. While present in pseudepigraphic literature, and common in patristic sources, this view is not found in the early Rabbis, see Ginzberg, *Legends*, v, 108 f.

[55] PL 6, 330 f. Quoted, with other relevant sources, by Emerson, pp. 918 f., and by Dexinger, pp. 99 f.

[56] Past research on this topic is reviewed by Anna Katharina Reither, *Das Motiv der 'neutralen Engel' in Wolframs 'Parzival'* (Inaugural-Dissertation Mainz, 1965), especially pp. 12–29. Samuel Singer has repeatedly drawn attention in this context to the Book of Enoch and the myth of the lustful angels, e.g. in 'Zu Wolframs Parzival' (1898), pp. 363 ff. and in 'Dogma und Dichtung des Mittelalters', *PMLA*, 62 (1947), 867 ff. — in part forestalled by San-Marte, '*Parcival'-Studien*, II, pp. 57 ff. — but the suggestion has never been fully exploited. It is however generally accepted that the motif is of legendary origin, see Reither, p. 28 and Bruno Nardi, 'Gli angeli che non furon ribelli nè fur fedeli a Dio', *Lectura Dantis Siciliana* (1959), pp. 1–24.

[57] Dexinger, pp. 103 ff.

[58] Medieval punctuation could easily lead to these statements being linked. Even in a modern edition this reading cannot be ruled out. Wittkower, p. 175, note 2, points to a tradition which identified the cynocephali with the giants. Pliny, *Nat. Hist.*, VII, 2, 32, attributes the genesis of monstrous peoples to 'ingeniosa . . . natura', cf. *Reinfrid*'s reference to 'nâtûre' as the helpmate of Adam (19715).

[59] The Book of Jubilees speaks of three classes of giants (7.22), while in 1 Enoch, 7. 5 the giants sin against birds, beasts, reptiles and fish, cf. 86.4 where elephants, camels, and asses (the three classes of giant?) arise from the union of stars (=Watchers) with oxen (=Cainites). Easily misinterpreted statements like that of Sulpicius Severus, *Historia Sacra*, 1.2: '. . . humanam corrupere [cf. *misserietent*!] progeniem: ex quorum coitu Gigantes editi esse dicuntur, cum diversæ inter se naturæ permixtio monstra gigneret' (PL 20, 97A), quoted by Emerson,

p. 924, also perhaps gave rise to a view of greater generality. See further *The Babylonian Talmud, Sanhedrin,* p. 740; the corruption of the generation of the Flood 'caused beasts and animals, animals and beasts to copulate; and all of these were brought in connection with man, and man with them all'. *Midrash Rabbah,* Genesis, I, p. 196: [From Adam to Enosh men were created in the image of God] 'but from then onwards Centaurs were created' . . . 'men's faces became ape-like, and they became vulnerable to demons', cf. p. 203 and pp. 228 f. (miscegenation, see Gen. VI, 12). According to *Midrash Rabbah,* Genesis, I, 213 f., the generation of the Flood was blotted out for legalizing unions with animals and for pederasty, cf. J. Preuss, *Biblisch-talmudische Medizin* (Berlin, 1911), pp. 584 f.

[60] James Carney, 'The Irish Elements in *Beowulf*', *Studies in Irish Literature and History* (Dublin, 1955), p. 103. Zarncke, *Der Priester Johannes,* I, pp. 910–11: the creatures encountered in the realm of Prester John include 'lamiae . . . homines agrestes, [homines cornuti], fauni, satiri . . . pigmei, cenocephali, gygantes, quorum altitudo est quadraginta cubitorum, [monoculi], cyclopes et avis, quae vocatur fenix'.

[61] In drawing attention to this passage, S. J. Crawford, 'Grendel's Descent from Cain', *MLR,* 24 (1929), 63, has overlooked the reference to it by S. Bugge, 'Studien über das *Beowulfepos*', *Beiträge,* 12 (1887), 82. The latter already points to the error *cames* for *caines* in the Beowulf MS., line 107, see also Carney, p. 102, note 1. Bugge also concludes: 'Die Vorstellung, daß die Unholde von Cain stammen, lernten die Angelsachsen vielleicht zunächst von den Irländern kennen' (p. 82).

[62] Op. cit., p. 107. On p. 114 Carney fails to recognize the origin of the story that two columns survive the Flood.

[63] See note 42, p. 34, above, and Fr. Klaeber, 'Die christlichen Elemente im *Beowulf,* II', *Anglia,* 35 (1912), 259–63. Some of the more recent literature is listed in J. L. Baird, 'Grendel the Exile', *Neuphilologische Mitteilungen,* 67 (1966), 375–81. R. E. Kaske, '*Beowulf* and the Book of Enoch', *Speculum,* 46 (July 1971), 421–31, makes a tentative case for a broader contribution of I Enoch to 'the cosmos assumed by the poet of *Beowulf*' (p. 431). Kaske points to the probability that I Enoch was available in England in Latin translation during the eighth century (p. 423). Charles Donahue, '*Beowulf* and Christian Tradition: A Reconsideration from a Celtic Stance', *Traditio,* 21 (1965), 55–116, considers that 'the ecclesiastical material and doctrine behind *Beowulf* was. . . ultimately derived from Irish missionaries' (p. 80). This ecclesiastical material included much of Eastern origin (pp. 66 f. and note 38), or otherwise known only in Eastern texts, cf. K. H. Jackson, *The International Popular Tale and Early Welsh Tradition* (Cardiff, 1961), p. 120. For the presence of Oriental monks (and possibly sculptors) in early Ireland see Françoise Henry, *Irish Art in the Early Christian Period (to 800 A.D.),* revised edition (London, 1965), pp. 64 and 133.

[64] See Emerson, pp. 871 f. and 878 ff.; Ginzberg, *Legends,* I, 10 ff.; I, 113 ff.; V, 143: 'the *Zohar* conceives the Cainites as a species of genii, demons, and monsters'.

[65] *Beowulf,* edited by Fr. Klaeber, third edition (Boston, 1950). English translation D. Wright, Penguin Classics (1963).

[66] *De origine actibusque Getarum,* MGH, Auct. Ant., V, i, edited by Th. Mommsen (Berlin, 1882), XXIV, 121–2. I am indebted to Dr George Gillespie for this reference.

[67] *Sanct Brandan. Ein lateinischer und drei deutsche Texte,* edited by Carl Schröder (Erlangen, 1871), pp. 78 ff.; see also pp. 147 ff. and 185 ff. Singer, 'Dogma und Dichtung', pp. 867 f., points in this context to the later version of the legend in which the neutral angels have been transformed into swine-headed monsters. Singer associates the 'fabelhafte Häßlichkeit' of Cundrîe and Malcrêatiure, 'vor allem ihr borstiges Haar' with the angels in this transformation. More dubious is his attempt to equate Wolfram's 'templeise' with the neutral angels (p. 867), cf.

the comments of J. Bumke, *Die Wolfram von Eschenbach Forschung seit 1945. Bericht und Bibliographie* (Munich, 1970), p. 263.

[68] See already San-Marte, *Parcival-Studien*, II, pp. 87 f., who also establishes the connexion with Gen. VI. 1–7; likewise Hagen, *Der Gral*, pp. 14 ff., who, however, lays undue stress on the legend of Prester John as a source. W. Snelleman, *Das Haus Anjou und der Orient in Wolframs 'Parzival'* (Ph.D. Dissertation, University of Amsterdam, Nijkerk, 1941), pp. 178 ff., accurately states the affiliation to the fabulous peoples but within an untenably narrow frame of reference.

[69] Chrétien de Troyes, *Le Roman de Perceval ou Le Conte du Graal*, edited by W. Roach, second edition (Geneva and Paris, 1959).

[70] For the most recent treatment of this figure see the relevant section in Marion E. Gibbs, *wîplîchez wîbes reht. A Study of the Women Characters in the Works of Wolfram von Eschenbach*, Duquesne Studies, Philological Series, 15 (Pittsburgh, 1972). This work is concerned largely with ethical values, however, and does not probe deeply into the origin of the character, any more than does F. R. Knapp, 'Die häßliche Gralsbotin und die victorinische Ästhetik', *Sprachkunst. Beiträge zur Literaturwissenschaft*, 3 (1972), 1–10. The most penetrating recent study of Cundrîe on the latter level is that by H. Kolb, *Munsalvaesche. Studien zum Kyotproblem* (Munich, 1963), pp. 36–50, see the discussion of individual issues in later footnotes. The name 'Cundrîe' is treated on pp. 36–7. Kolb's analysis of Wolfram's attitude to this character (pp. 40 ff.) is a useful counter-weight to the less critical view advanced by Gibbs.

[71] Seitz, *Die Darstellung häßlicher Menschen*, pp. 11 f.

[72] Snelleman, pp. 179 f. rightly quotes *Parz.*, 313.21: 'si was genaset als ein hunt' as evidence, but does not see the wider implications of the fact that Wolfram has made his two characters 'zu indischen Kynokephaloi'. See however page 37, note 68 above, and Seitz, pp. 63 ff.: 'Aus dem deutschen *Lucidarius* übernahm Wolfram die Verbindung von Exotenhäßlichkeit mit dem Adamstöchtermythos'. Phyllis Ackerman, 'Who is Kundrie — What is She?', *The Literary Review*, 2 (Teaneck, New Jersey, 1959), 458–68, considers, implausibly, that Cundrîe is modelled on an Egyptian (and Cretan) goddess, Epet Ta-ueret, a semi-humanized hippopotamus, sometimes depicted with lion-feet, who represented the constellation Boötes, cf. Bumke, p. 303.

[73] For a description of the work see D. J. A. Ross, *Alexander Historiatus. A Guide to Medieval Illustrated Alexander Literature*, Warburg Institute Surveys, 1 (London, 1963), pp. 32–3. For the texts and a study of them, see E. Faral, 'Une source latine de l'Histoire d'Alexandre: La Lettre sur les merveilles de l'Inde', *Romania*, 43 (1914), 199–215 and 353–70. The quotations here (from Latin Redaction D) are drawn from A. Hilka, 'Ein neuer (altfranzösischer) Text des Briefes über die Wunder Asiens', *Zeitschrift für französische Sprache und Literatur*, 46, i (1920), 92–103.

[74] Faral, p. 367.

[75] Edition in A. Hilka, *Der altfranzösische Prosa-Alexanderroman* (Halle, 1920), p. 179.

[76] See M. R. James, *Marvels of the East* (Oxford, 1929). The earliest of the three manuscripts he reproduces, Vitellius A. XV (British Museum), dates from about A.D. 1000, but the underlying picture-cycle is believed to derive from a continental archetype. For our purpose it is of great interest to note that the *Marvels of the East* section is flanked in Vitellius A. XV by the legend of St Christopher (the dog-headed saint, see below), by Alexander's letter to Aristotle — and by *Beowulf* (see James, Introduction, p. 1).

[77] A later variant is that they possess hairy bodies, see the section on Cynocephali in the article 'Fabelwesen' by Salome Zajadacz-Hastenrath, *Reallexikon zur deutschen Kunstgeschichte*, VI (Stuttgart, 1971), 739 ff.

[78] See Ross, *Illustrated Medieval Alexander-Books*, pp. 63–4 and Fig. 60, cf.

Figs. 399 and 400. Ross notes the interesting confusion between Cynocephali, dog-heads, and Equinocephali, horse-heads (p. 63, note 17), cf. the quotation from the *Sex Aetates Mundi*, above, p. 18. *Ein deutsches Adambuch*, ed. Vollmer, pp. 26–7, describes, in a passage attributed to Methodius, but largely derived from Wolfram, how Adam warned his daughters against certain herbs. Some disregarded the warning: 'etlich gewan rosshawbt, etlich ainen langen zand als ain wildes eberswein, etlichs an hawbt, den stuenden dy augen an der prust, etlichs het nwer ainen fues. dicz geschah von der beiber glust vnd von virbicz, als sümlich noch hewt tuent.'

[79] My references to the Cynocephali are not intended to rule out influence by other encounters, e.g. with giant women hunters, 'habentes corpora magna, barbas usque ad mammas, capita plana, vestitae pellibus', *Priester Johannes*, ed. Zarncke, p. 911 (= *Letter of Pharasmanes*, D, xxi). See the illustrations in Ross, *Illustrated Medieval Alexander-Books*, Figs. 56 and 397.

[80] The descriptions of heathen warriers cited by Kolb, *Munsalvaesche*, pp. 39 f., from French sources, provide characteristic examples of this influence. Kolb remarks merely: 'die Häßlichkeit im Orient beheimateter Menschen ... [ist] in der damaligen Dichtung ein literarischer Topos' (p. 42) and refers to the *Annolied*. One may recall here that direct knowledge of aspects of the Alexander legend has often been posited for Wolfram in other contexts, for instance that of the Grail stone.

[81] Edited by W. Foerster, 4th edition, Romanische Bibliothek, 5 (Halle, 1912). Hartmann von Aue, *Iwein*, edited by G. F. Benecke und K. Lachmann, revised by L. Wolff, seventh edition, 1, Text (Berlin, 1968).

[82] Barbara Seitz provides a detailed comparison of the two figures (pp. 6–9), pointing out the contrasting intentions of the two authors and supplying some comparative material; however, the overall problem of such descriptions cannot be approached adequately without access to a broader spectrum of evidence than she considers. Herbert Kolb, *Munsalvaesche*, pp. 38 ff., adduces many illuminating parallels, above all from the *Chansons de Geste*, but does not analyse them in any great detail or place them in a broad enough context. None listed suffice for an explanation of more than individual elements of Cundrîe's appearance, cf. the reference to 'Hundsköpfe', p. 39, note 169.

[83] Seitz, pp. 7–8, rightly refers to the presence 'des Riesischen und Rassisch-Exotischen' in both authors, but means by the latter the statement 'qui ressan-bloit mor' (*Yvain*, 288). Kolb, *Munsalvaesche*, p. 46, on the other hand sensitively detects both heathen origin and 'Abkunft von den Giganten'.

[84] See *Wiener Genesis*, 655 ff., blackness of the children of Cain. Early Christian exegesis and much of medieval literature in associating black men with the devil and blackness with sin, see D. A. Wells, 'The Middle Dutch *Moriaen*, Wolfram von Eschenbach's *Parzival*, and Medieval Tradition', *Studia Neerlandica* (1971), 261–8, with valuable reference to recent literature on this subject.

[85] 'Owein' or 'Chwedyl Iarlles y Ffynnawn', edited by R. L. Thomson (Dublin, 1968), p. 5, 109–10: 'ac vn troet yssyd idaw, ac vn llygat yg knewillyn y tal'; translation by G. and T. Jones, *The Mabinogion*, Everyman's Library, 97 (London, 1968). A. I. Tyndale, 'A Re-Examination of Celtic Tradition in the Romance of *Yvain* by Chrestiens de Troyes' (unpublished M.Litt. dissertation, University of Cambridge, 1971), p. 58 does not realize the connexion with the fabulous peoples. A. H. Krappe, 'The Grail Messenger', *Philological Quarterly*, 26 (1947), 352–7, refers appositely to the influence of the Loathly Lady tradition on the depiction of the Grail Messenger, although he does not notice Wolfram's characteristic divergences from this tradition. He does, however, point (p. 354 and note 9) to the affinities between Leborcham, a slave woman in King Conchobar's household, whose heels faced forward and knees backwards, and who travelled throughout Ireland in a day, with the description of an exotic race in Pliny,

VII. 2; add Isidor, *Etymologies*, XI. iii, 24. This affinity is overlooked by H. Güntert, *Kundry*, Germanische Bibliothek. Untersuchungen und Texte, 25 (Heidelberg, 1928), pp. 23–4, who draws the same parallel with Leborcham, and observes that she, like Cundrîe, is unfree (*Parz.*, 519.2 ff.), eloquent, and a 'surziere'. Güntert's interpretation of Cundrîe as 'Botin aus dem Totenland' (p. 36) is untenably onesided, however, even if some aspects of it (demonic affiliations) could easily be reconciled with the view advanced in this article.

[86] M. Haupt, *Opuscula*, II (Leipzig, 1876), p. 244, 27. This view is established already by Pliny and his forerunners, e.g. Ktesias, cf. *Nat. Hist.*, VII, ii, 21: 'Praecipue India Aethiopumque tractus miraculis scatent. maxima in India gignuntur animalia', and is naturally taken for granted in the *Letter of Alexander to Aristotle* on the wonders of India, edited by Fr. Pfister, *Kleine Texte zum Alexanderroman* (Heidelberg, 1910), pp. 21 ff. This text contains a reference (p. 36) to composite monsters with swine's head, lion's tail, and clawed feet. Griffins are found with these creatures, while hairy women are encountered shortly afterwards. The priest of the Trees of the Sun and Moon is of giant stature, 'habebat nigrum corpus, dentes caninos' (p. 33), see Ross, *Illustrated Medieval Alexander-Books*, Figs. 205, 233–4, 352 (animal-headed), etc.

[87] Compare Pliny, *Nat. Hist.*, VI, xxii, 68: 'But almost the whole of the peoples of India . . . are surpassed in power and glory by the Prasi, with the very large and wealthy city of Patna ("amplissima urbe ditissimaque Palibothra"), from which some peoples give the name of Palibothri to the race itself, and indeed to the whole tract of country from the Ganges.' Tusked, shock-haired anti-gods (demons) are today still a feature of the folklore of India and Ceylon. The attempt of H. Goetz, 'Der Orient der Kreuzzüge in Wolframs *Parzival*', *Archiv für Kulturgeschichte*, 49 (1967), 1–42, to trace Cundrîe and Malcrêatiure back to 'niedere Hindu-Gottheiten' (p. 23) is thus not totally misguided, but only indicates something close to the *ultimate origin* of this iconography.

[88] See Singer, 'Dogma und Dichtung', p. 870: 'Der Name stammt aus Solin, resp. Plinius, wo eine riesengroße Araberin so genannt wird: der Verbindung der Engel mit den Menschen entstammen ja die Riesen.'

[89] The antecedents and nature of Cundrîe and Malcrêatiure are clearly recognized by Kolb, *Munsalvaesche*, pp. 36 ff., who includes references to the Book of Enoch, the children of Cain, *Beowulf*, the fabulous peoples and other matters central to the present essay. Much of this material, however, he shares with earlier Germanistic (and Anglistic) research. His preoccupation with the Kyot problem appears to have led him to the origin of the giants through Romanistic sources like W. W. Comfort, 'The Literary Rôle of the Saracens in the French Epic', *PMLA*, 55 (1940) and caused him to overlook relevant studies nearer to hand. The present essay, while coinciding with Kolb's argumentation in some important particulars, differs from him on very many issues, above all in concluding that Wolfram knew of the Cainite origin of Cundrîe and her brother — Kolb accepts this (p. 44) for either Wolfram or for a predecessor followed by him (Kyot?) — and that, instead of wishing to undermine this origin (Kolb, p. 44), he heightens the poetic scope of *Parzival* by exploiting it to the full. There are no grounds whatever for considering that Kyot may have supplied the story of Adam's daughters (Kolb, p. 45), which is attested primarily on German soil (see above). Here, too, Kyot, as a connected source, proves to be a fiction, cf. now C. Lofmark, 'Wolfram's Source References in *Parzival*', *MLR*, 67 (1972), 820–44.

[90] Edited by A. B. Friedman and N. T. Harrington, Early English Text Society, 254 (London, 1964), l. 559, and note pp. 116 f. This passage is quoted by Emerson, pp. 885 f. with further examples. *Kyng Alisaunder*, edited by G. V. Smithers, EETS, 227 (London, 1952): The troops with Darius include (B 1932) 'of Saba þe duk Mauryn/(He was of Kaymes kynrede . . .); his men are Cynocephali.

[91] Like Adam, who is sometimes seen as the inaugurator of the Seven Liberal Arts (see above). Cf. also Kolb, *Munsalvaesche*, p. 37. A command of all languages is attributed to certain fabulous beings in the *Letter of Pharasmanes*.

[92] Compare Snelleman, *Das Haus Anjou*, p. 154.

[93] See Schwietering, 'Natur und *art*', p. 465.

[94] See, for example, Fr. Zarncke, *Der Priester Johannes*, p. 839,23: Per medium cuius Physon, unus de paradisi fluminibus, limpidissimis emanat aquis, aurum preciosissimum atque gemmas preciosissimas foras emittens, unde Indicae regiones opulentissimae fiunt.

[95] See Snelleman, pp. 157 ff. and W. Deinert, *Ritter und Kosmos*, pp. 104-5 and passim. Deinert shows convincingly that *Parz.*, 518.5 ff. (powers of Adam) reflects the belief that knowledge of the 'virtues' of the planets is necessary for a true understanding of the herbs, since the two are interdependent.

[96] Deinert, pp. 104 ff.

[97] Deinert, pp. 112-14. Clinschor, incidentally, maintains obscure relations with 'Feirefîzes landen' in the East. Through Orgeluse he obtains possession of the mysterious 'krâmgewant' given to Anfortas by Secundille, from whom he has illicitly taken (592. 18) the unique, richly-jewelled 'Wundersäule', the basis of his power.

[98] See for example P. E. Beichner, *The Medieval Representative of Music, Jubal or Tubalcain?* (Notre Dame, Indiana, 1954).

[99] It is no coincidence that Wolfram employs a humility formula at this point, naming Hercules and Alexander among those more qualified to pronounce on the stones adorning the armour than himself; both figures are associated in the medieval mind with India.

[100] See Emerson, *Legends of Cain*, pp. 915-16 and 928-9.

[101] *De Cultu Foeminarum*, PL 1, 1305C: 'Nam cum et [angeli] materias quasdam bene occultas, et artes plerasque non bene revelatas, sæculo multo magis imperito prodidissent (siquidem et metallorum opera nudaverant, et herbarum ingenia traduxerant, et incantationum vires provulgaverant, et omnem curiositatem, usque ad stellarum interpretationem designaverant) proprie et quasi peculiariter fœminis instrumentum istud muliebris gloriæ contulerunt (i.e. jewellery and cosmetics)'. Instead, Tertullian advocates humility and chastity.

[102] In this very special sense, Güntert, *Kundry*, pp. 29 ff., has some justification for drawing the parallel with 'Frau Welt' (and the Babylonian Whore!). In every other respect these analogies are wholly misconceived, cf. the hostile comment by Deinert, p. 114, note 1.

[103] Kolb, 'Isidorsche "Etymologien" ', p. 117, wisely leaves aside the question of whether Wolfram gained his knowledge of Isidor direct or through intermediaries. See too Chr. Gerhardt, 'Wolframs Adlerbild *Willehalm*, 189, 2-24', *Zeitschrift für deutsches Altertum*, 99 (1970), p. 218: 'Ich möchte darüber hinaus auch die Frage offen lassen, ob Wolfram überhaupt aus einer gelehrten Quelle oder aus dem aus gelehrter Wurzel stammenden Konversationsgut der Zeit geschöpft hat.' In the same way, no knowledge is assumed for Wolfram in the present article, which could not have been acquired in the (basically oral) manner postulated for him by H. Grundmann, 'Dichtete Wolfram von Eschenbach am Schreibtisch?', *Archiv für Kulturgeschichte*, 49 (1967), 391-405.

[104] By comparing Cundrîe's appearance unfavourably with 'bêâ schent' (313.3), Wolfram opens the way to an unfavourable interpretation, cf. 658.26 ff., where Clinschor is said to have power over 'mal unde bêâ schent, / die zwischen dem firmament / wonent unt der erden zil'. This is possibly yet another element of the narrative intended to keep the audience in a state of uncertainty, which is only gradually resolved in Cundrîe's favour.

[105] See Z. Ameisenowa, 'Animal-Headed Gods, Evangelists, Saints and Righteous Men', *Journal of the Warburg and Courtauld Institutes*, 12 (1949), 21-45 (pp. 34 ff.).

[106] See *Analecta Bollandiana*, I (1882), 123: εἰ γὰρ ἐκ τοῦ γένους τῶν κυνοκεφάλων ὑπῆρχεν, γῆς δὲ τῶν ἀνθρωποφάγων. In the Latin version preserved in an eleventh-century French MS. this passage reads: 'Quidam autem vir, cum esset alienigena, regionis eorum qui homines manducabant, qui habebat terribilem visionem et quasi canino capite . . . (*Analecta Bollandiana*, x (1891), 395). The iconography of St Christopher as a dog-head was probably widespread in Byzantine art from the tenth century, but is not found in the West, cf. H. Aurenhammer, *Lexikon der christlichen Ikonographie*, I (Vienna, this fasc. 1965), 435 ff., with bibliography, and L. Réau, *Iconographie de l'Art Chrétien*, III, I (Paris, 1958), 304. The *Martyrologium* of Usuardus, a Zwiefalten MS. of *c.* 1140 (Stuttgart, Landesbibliothek, Cod. hist. fol. 415, fol. 50 shows a giant lion(?)-headed St Christopher.

[107] Quoted by A. R. Anderson, *Alexander's Gate, Gog and Magog, And the Inclosed Nations*, Monographs of the Medieval Academy of America, 5 (Cambridge, Massachusetts, 1932), p. 48.

[108] Anderson, p. 88. In the continuation of the passage quoted the Anthropophagi are named. Not only are the Huns, believed by Jordanes to stem from demons (see above), often associated with Gog and Magog: Attila himself can be portrayed as dog-headed (Réau, *Iconographie*, III, I, 307).

[109] See Marcelle Thiébaux, 'The Mouth of the Boar as a Symbol in Medieval Literature', *Romance Philology*, 22 (1969), 281–99; Janson, *Apes and Ape Lore*, pp. 13–27 (the ape as 'figura diaboli', persisting until the thirteenth century and even later). The lion and bear also contribute to the iconography of demons, while blackness and shagginess is associated *inter alia* with the devil and is interpreted as an image of sin; bristling hair can indicate demonic bestiality, see L. Réau, *Iconographie*, II, I (Paris, 1956), 57 ff. Cain is sometimes depicted with horns, or as covered with hair, Emerson, p. 873. H. R. Jauss, 'Die klassische und die christliche Rechtfertigung des Häßlichen in mittelalterlicher Literatur', in *Die nicht mehr schönen Künste, Grenzphänomene des Ästhetischen*, edited by H. R. Jauss (Munich, 1968), pp. 143–68, asserts of medieval art; 'Wo immer in ihr menschliche und tierische Gestalt gemischt erscheinen, ist damit das gegenbildlich Dämonische bedeutet' (save for certain fairy-like creatures of Arthurian Romance 'imported' from Celtic mythology, p. 154). He appears unaware of the background explored in the present essay, when discussing examples from the Chansons de Geste. F. P. Knapp, op. cit., p. 9, speaks of Cundrîe's 'infernalische(r) Häßlichkeit'. On the allegorical interpretation of animals in general, see D. Schmidtke, *Geistliche Tierinterpretation in der deutschsprachigen Literatur des Mittelalters* (1100–1500), dissertation, F. U. Berlin, 1968; p. 208 ff. 'Auslegungen auf den Teufel' — relatively unrewarding for our purpose.

[110] Compare the straightforward, unadulterated description of Cynocephali in Wolfram's *Willehalm*, 35.10 ff.: King Margot, whose second land is Orkeise, which lies at the Eastern extremity of the world, was accompanied by King Gorhant: 'bî der Ganjas (*addition by Wolfram!*) was des lant. / des volc was vor und hinden horn, / âne menschlîch stimme erkorn: / der dôn von ir munde / gal sam die leithunde / oder als ein kelber muoter lüet'; noted already by S. Singer, *Wolframs 'Willehalm'* (Bern, 1918), pp. 16 f.; Wolfram is under the influence of his French source here, although without following it slavishly.

[111] On Parzival as new Adam, see Deinert, pp. 56 ff.

[112] The interpretation of *ungenuht* assumed here differs from that put forward by L. P. Johnson, 'Ungenuht al eine (*Parzival*, 782,23)', in *Probleme mittelalterlicher Überlieferung und Textkritik*, edited by P. F. Ganz and W. Schröder (Berlin, 1968), pp. 49-66, see the paraphrase proposed on p. 64.

[113] Deinert, p. 55.

[114] Characteristically, Charles, II, pp. 200 f. See also Emerson, pp. 863 and 883.

4

Lanzelet and the Queens

By ROSEMARY N. COMBRIDGE

TITLES of papers are funny things. When I was asked to read a paper to the Institute of Germanic Studies, I had been cogitating vaguely on what Ulrich von Zatzikhoven's *Lanzelet*[1] might all be about, and I offered to 'stick my neck out on *Lanzelet*'. I shall in fact be sticking other people's necks out rather than my own, because various unpublished theses, including a recent French one based on less vague cogitations, are very germane to my subject.[2] I decided to put the queens into my title as an indication of what I regard as one of the keys to the poem. I did not name Ulrich in the title, because the French (or probably Anglo-Norman) romance he is adapting not being extant, nor any other adaptation of it, we usually have no means of determining what is Ulrich's own contribution. We have to accept that the narrator of whom we may speak is a composite person, Ulrich *and* the author of the source-romance, and that any artistic *intention* which we may infer from a study of the text is not necessarily one individual's intention: the notion of 'intention' must here more than ever be used as a critic's rationalization, not as the psychological reality of the poet. The omission of Ulrich does not mean that I propose talking about Chrétien's idiosyncratic and largely divergent treatment of the Lancelot story.[3]

Rehabilitation is a current fashion in literary criticism, and it has a momentum which is only surpassed by that with which ever new periods or fields of collecting activity become fashionable in the world of antiques. The instances that have impressed themselves on my consciousness have been: the comparatively recent revival of interest in Baroque poetry; the discovery of the artistic autonomy of early Middle High German poetry, strikingly demonstrated by Ingeborg Schröbler's lecture in the Senate House some years ago; and the vindication of the formal coherence of the vast Medieval prose romances, by Professor Vinaver in his presidential address to the Modern Humanities Research Association in 1966.[4]

Since Professor Schröbler's lecture elucidating the principles of composition underlying *Vom Rechte*,[5] I have become gradually less able to read assessments of the type 'a formless concatenation of episodes' without wondering how long it will be before someone discovers the formal principle behind the work or genre in question. One need not go back to Ehrismann,[6] with his judgement that *Lanzelet* aims to 'entertain the audience by means of the strangeness of its happenings', or that Ulrich's source 'heaps up adventures and repetitious motifs without integrating them through the hero's character'; one need only read de Boor in 1960:[7] 'Ulrich, Hartmann's younger contemporary, shares his choice of an Arthurian subject, but never rises beyond the subject-matter' (abgleitend in reine Stofflichkeit), 'the only appeal of which is a certain down-to-earth vividness' (deren einziger Reiz eine gewisse handgreifliche Anschaulichkeit ist). And how I agreed with them! But it is bad for the morale to be long engaged in editing a work one finds artistically sterile; as a matter of self-preservation the mind gets to work on it and asks, 'Why this? Why that? What is such-and-such doing here?'. The critics I have quoted had yet a further reproach to make to the narrator: not only was the work superficial and incoherent: it lacked *problems*. Ehrismann: 'seelische Probleme kennt diese am Äußeren haftende Erzählungsweise nicht.' De Boor formulates his disappointment pungently: the griefless hero is the problemless hero: 'Lanzelet, der Held, der kein *trûren* kennt, er kennt auch keine Problematik.' As if it were not a sufficient task and destiny to rise from anonymity and a sub-chivalrous upbringing to quadruple exemplary kingship, without the poet's introducing *problems* into the bargain! And de Boor's boredom with *Lanzelet* made him overlook the fact that the hero *does* learn *trûren*! This may be an inconsistency in the narrative, and it is not explicitly pointed to as a development or change in Lanzelet's character by Ulrich, but it is nevertheless narrated. I have blamed de Boor's boredom, but it might also be in place to blame Ulrich's narrative art, because there is no point in trying to pretend that Ulrich is in the greatest line of poets. Even if the (with hindsight) archaic features in his diction are deliberate,[8] his style lacks the suppleness and richness and usually the evocativeness of Hartmann's, and his junctures and links are often awkward. But to compare him unfavourably with Hartmann as a stylist is one thing, to depreciate his story because its structure is not as streamlined nor its sense as plain as those of *Erec*, is another. (How long have we been able to talk of the 'sense' of *Erec*'s being *plain* to us?) It has often been observed that providing one assumes that the story is as it is because this will tell us what the poet wants to say, one can find as much profundity in Chrétien de Troyes as in his more moralizing imitators, Hartmann and Wolfram. 'Providing one assumes that the story is as it is because this will tell us what the poet wants to say': this is the assumption that W. J. Schröder has found so fruitful in interpreting *König Rother*[9] — but of course it will not work if one simultaneously assumes that a poem so unlike Hartmann's or Chrétien's in theme and structure as Ulrich's cannot be meant to say anything worth saying.[10] I am not thinking of Chrétien's *Chevalier de la charrete*, because Ulrich's theme is so different, but of his *Erec et Enide*[11] and *Yvain*.[12]

This is where Professor Vinaver's contrast of the single-stranded romance[13] favoured by Chrétien and appreciated by modern readers, and the many-stranded, closely-interwoven, open-ended prose romances, killed by Cervantes and rescued through metamorphosis into the modern form at the hands of Malory, can help us. The different threads in Lanzelet's life: his inherited royal destiny, the task laid upon him by his foster-mother the fairy Sea-Queen to avenge her on Iweret, the urge to vindicate his honour on the castle of Plûrîs where a dwarf strikes his horse and him with a whip as he sets out in search of knighthood, these three threads intertwine and enrich each other in a manner doubtless far simpler than that of the prose romances; but nevertheless the fact that there are three threads, that the reappearance of a motif does not only depend on the narrator's whim as in the reappearance of Guivreiz in *Erec*, but is *given* simply because Lanzelet sets out say, to accomplish the Plûrîs adventure and is distracted by the chance completion of the Iweret adventure, so that the Plûrîs theme is not complete and comes in again later, or because Lanzelet's discovery of his ancestry is made by his foster-mother to depend on the Iweret adventure, which as it turns out provides him with the royal consort he needs if he is to fulfil his hereditary function as ruler adequately — this givenness of multiplicity as a starting-point puts *Lanzelet*, to my mind, in Professor Vinaver's many-stranded category.

Once we see that Chrétien is not the criterion of structure,[14] we are free to see other things too. We no longer necessarily expect the sequence: premature glory, fall, rehabilitation, with which Chrétien has familiarized us and which may well be peculiar to him, as Professor Collas[15] has suggested. We are free to ask ourselves whether the connexion between events and their significance is the same as in Chrétien: Lanzelet's four liaisons are not distinguished in the form of their celebration, yet only the third, that with Iweret's daughter, Iblis, is life-long and is linked with his role as king of his own kingdom. Are the first two and the fourth only relics of an earlier version incompatible with the realities of dynastic monogamy, entertainment for an erotically self-conscious courtly audience whom a Chrétien and a Hartmann might woo in vain with their fusion of Eros and marriage, so long held apart by theologians and troubadours alike? Or have these other three manifestations of Lanzelet's popularity with women a structural function other than their value as episodes?[16] — Are the irrational elements in Lanzelet's life: his water-fairy foster-mother and her omniscience; the magic by which she renders all visitors to her cowardly son's castle worse cowards than himself in order to protect him, a magic to which Lanzelet ironically falls victim but which more ironically still results in his being commissioned by his captor to pursue his predatory neighbour Iweret, the enemy on whom he has promised to avenge his foster-mother; the sorcery of Malduc on which Arthur has to rely to rescue Guinevere from her perjured abductor: are these elements 'primitive' (meant as a value-judgement)? — Is the rescue of Lanzelet from Plûrîs by a ruse engineered by four Arthurian knights, and the second rescue of Guinevere by a combination of war, siege and sorcery instead of by single combat as on the first occasion, unworthy of the high, self-reliant valour of the 'real' Arthurian hero?

I have argued on another occasion[17] that the devoted team-spirit shown by the knights in *Lanzelet* in aiding each other and their overlord should be regarded as presenting a knightly ideal *as valid as* that of the more individualistic and introvert romances with which we are more familiar; what I like to call their 'infinite capacity for rallying round' is, ethically speaking, it seems to me by no means an outmoded virtue and the extent to which they can take their esprit de corps for granted is a political strength. — The problem of magic and its ability to make even Lanzelet withdrawn and lethargic, while still shame-conscious, cannot be satisfactorily solved at the realistic level. If one does not believe in magic and sees no evidence of its operation in the world, that is that. But formulate the question like this: which is more realistic: a world in which there are no obstacles that the hero cannot overcome, and none but human obstacles that the knights he defeats cannot overcome? or a world in which the unpredictable is openly accepted? in which the hero is not ashamed to owe part of his good fortune to a fairy Queen and in which he may meet and find himself helpless against forces beyond his own control? — then the artistic role of magic and other supernatural phenomena as, paradoxically, contributing to realism becomes clear. Chrétien largely internalizes the hostile forces as his hero's uxoriousness or his obsession with jousting, and rationalizes benevolent forces as the friendly lion — it is a matter of taste. (I have over-done this, I know; but it is a talking-point.)

If we now look again at Lanzelet's liaisons, seeing them too as it were *not* as representational art, what do we find? Up to and including the winning of Iblis, his queen, Lanzelet has each time stepped into the shoes of his lady's father or guardian, and inherited him. René Perennec regards the acquisition of power by marriage, exemplified in Lanzelet's first three liaisons, as one of the attractions which the Anglo-Norman poem would have had for contemporaries, among whom were count-less younger sons who must have aspired to just such a goal. At the realistic level, these episodes pose a number of moral problems in the conduct of the young ladies concerned, for encouraging, in the first case indeed for actively wooing, the hero, knowing the risks he and their respective fathers or uncle run. Of course the situations are complex: two are instances of the tyranny of love, Minne, one is motivated by the father's oppressive-ness towards his daughter, another by the uncle's un-knightly treatment of the knight-errant hero for slaying his chief counsellor in a combat brought about by the visitor's ignorance of local bye-laws; two of the lords concerned run an adventure for all comers which is asking for trouble; and the ladies, as Perennec has pointed out, are graded in sensitivity, Iblis, Lanzelet's future queen, being the most aware of the conflict of loyalties, actively anxious to prevent the combat by elopement, and conveniently fainting for the whole course of the combat so that Ulrich does not have to decide how she would have behaved had she seen it. Ulrich does his best, according to M. Perennec, to exculpate Iblis in particular. This problem ends here, because Lanzelet's fourth mistress has no guardian.[18]

A feature common to the guardians of Lanzelet's first three conquests is their tyrannical bent, a characteristic they share with Lanzelet's father, Pant. I have spoken of Lanzelet's hereditary function in life. His station is that of a king's son, born to be king. The preoccupation of the Medieval aristocracy with all aspects of inheritance is well exemplified in German literature. There are romances such as *König Rother*, where wooing is the central theme because of the importance of providing a dynastic heir to the kingship. The situation at the opening of *König Rother* or half-way through Gottfried's *Tristan*, where the king's advisers counsel marriage and debate as to who would make their lord a suitable partner, is so common as to be capable of parody and inversion as at the end of *Der arme Heinrich*, where a nobleman marries a free peasant girl out of gratitude and unwordliness, thus effectively frustrating the dynastic aspect of the whole business.[19] In Hartmann's *Gregorius* and Gottfried's *Tristan* and their sources, the destiny of the hero is foreshadowed by that of his parents; moreover these heroes, like Lanzelet, inherit something of their father's character; Gregorius the love of chivalry proper to his station, *and* the willingness to settle down too soon and too near home, his Achilles' heel; Tristan shows something of his father's youthful impetuosity in his pursuit of his father's overlord and slayer; and Lanzelet has a reputation, even at the end of the poem, for standing no nonsense, while his desertion of his first lady-love is motivated by his resentment at her having made advances to him only after being rebuffed by his two older companions who had stood down when her father asked which of the three should have the honour of visiting the ladies before dinner. *Lanzelet* does *not* share with *Gregorius* and with the version of the Tristan-legend mentioned the feature of having a pre-history, the history of the parents, attached, such as Wolfram developed for *Parzival* on his own initiative without Chrétien's having set the example; the German fondness for the attached parental history I take to be due in part to the special German emphasis on the necessity of knightly *birth* for membership of a gradually closing aristocracy,[20] and to the rigidity of the feudal hierarchy within the aristocracy itself,[21] but in part to factors which presumably operated in France as well: the growing popularity of lives of the Virgin as a preliminary to the life of Christ, and — appropriate in particular to the French version of the pseudo-legend of Pope Gregorius[22] — a certain fascination with the doctrine of original sin.[23] Gregorius, Tristan, Parzival, and Lanzelet all seem to inherit from their fathers, among more positive characteristics, a weakness, which they overcome by a characteristic of which it is difficult to say whether it is inherited from their mother or learned from their educator: a few slight touches suggest the second. Gregorius wins through with piety — which his mother has — reinforced by theology, which she has once had but which has evaporated under the shock of her second and this time unconscious incest; in Tristan's case his *destiny* is not determined by a characteristic at all, really, but his ultimate loyalty in love, and the diplomacy which stands him in such good stead in the details of living though it is powerless against Love herself, are both found incipiently in his mother who dies giving birth to him, and outstandingly in his guardian, Rual. Parzival's loyalty to Condwiramurs, the sympathy which lies dormant beneath his hobbledehoy exterior, and his gradually developing religious concern, may perhaps be said to be inherited from his mother and released by Gurnemanz and Trevrizent, while Lanzelet's insistence on his rights is tempered and balanced by the benevolence expected of an overlord by his subjects, characteristic of his mother Clârîne, whose kindliness postpones for many a day the revolt of Pant's subjects in which Pant is killed; this benevolence and patience, if they are inherited, are reinforced by the training Lanzelet receives at the hands of his rescuer from the revolt, the Queen of the water-fairies, at whose entirely female court he learns forbearance by learning never to resent a woman's jest, and by the example of King Arthur's openhandedness towards and care for the knights of his kingdom. Even at the last, when Lanzelet has taken possession of his father's kingdom and the kingdoms devolving on his wife from Iweret, he lives a life inspired by Arthur's advice (9410).

As in *Parzival*, and more than in *Erec* or *Iwein*, the whole of life is seen in *Lanzelet* as a quest,[24] until the hero has attained a state of true and safe equilibrium. Even then, he remains active in knightly pursuits essential to preserve this equilibrium. The tasks imposed by life appear in the form of quests. Knighthood, inevitably involving taking up his position as his father's heir, is Lanzelet's primary quest: the first task imposed on him by life is that he should fill adequately the station to which he was born. This would need no emphasizing to a Medieval audience. Having learned how to behave in society, and undergone an athletic training from sea-monsters at the Fairy Queen's command, Lanzelet desires to set out in search of knightly deeds, but when the Queen refuses to reveal his identity, he makes his identity an object of his quest, and readily accepts the duty of avenging his rescuer and guardian on her enemy Iweret as a condition of attaining to knowledge of his own identity. Lanzelet's instinctive yearning for the congenial activity of knighthood is, like that of Gregorius and Parzival, so strong that considerations of duty have no part to play at this stage, though we soon find him responsibly refusing an invitation to Arthur's court because he is not yet a seasoned knight and would be out of place in such company. The second quest, the quest for Iweret, appears to be felt by Lanzelet as an extension of the first, yet it involves willing acceptance of a responsibility sought and chosen as little as that imposed by birth, and Lanzelet, though having no choice, explicitly accepts the unwelcome limitation of anonymity until the task shall be fulfilled. These two quests, imposed on Lanzelet by life from the outset, highlight the difference between the Medieval notion of the journey through life and later notions. This is no yearning for the 'wide world' as opening up undreamt-of possibilities of escape from cow-herding or crossing-sweeping, nor is it a wish to stretch oneself, to discover the gifts and powers of a new and distinct personage whose heredity can tell one nothing. To which one should add promptly, to balance the picture, that presumably even in the Middle Ages those who were born to cow-herding had their dreams of a wide world as an escape from present reality, and that such may have come down to us in many a fairy-tale, and *one* certainly *has* come down to us, though from a critical angle, in the satirical story of *Meier Helmbrecht*.

So Lanzelet's ultimate task is to step into his father's shoes; to do this he has to win knowledge of his identity through discharging a debt of gratitude to the Water Queen. Setting out to fulfil these tasks, he acquires a third: that of avenging his own honour, real in spite of his lack of a name, on the castle of Plûrîs where the

dwarf has struck him. This last and the search for knighthood and his identity are what he consciously pursues;
the Fairy Queen has told him he will find Iweret if he lives
worthily, so he does not have to look for him. After he
has been initiated into the rudimentary knightly skills by
Johfrit de Liez, as Parzival was by Gurnemanz, Lanzelet's
first action is to end a combat between two exhausted
knights by threatening to help the one whose opponent
refuses to lay down his arms: his view of knighthood is
already governed by the principle of moderation: he
expresses his surprise at their having fought so im-
moderately, 'sô ze unmâzen' (699) — this is in keeping
with his early, spontaneous remark to Johfrit that if all
knights were as courteous as Johfrit he can't think why
they should ever want to fight each other. It is as a result
of thus preventing excessive fighting between two
knights that Lanzelet, seeking shelter along with them
for the night, stumbles on his first amorous adventure,
that of the pressing young woman who is inflamed with
love owing to her father's prohibition to her to marry,
who puts Lanzelet third on her list because she woos
the knights in the order in which they are lying, and
whose father Lanzelet kills next morning after being
challenged by him to a knife-throwing competition,
the deadly purpose of which is all too obvious. The
irony of it is that it was Lanzelet who encouraged his
companions to accept Galagandreiz's hospitality when
they were reluctant because Galagandreiz was known to
be vindictive, and Lanzelet trusted his own courtliness,
which he learned in the Fairy Queen's island palace
and which makes him more than ready to accept the
young lady's overtures.

For a time Lanzelet stays at this castle, but unlike
Gregorius,[25] only for a time, for, says Ulrich, he recalled

the purpose of his journey: 'sich bedâhte der helt balt /
durch waz er ûz was geriten' (1362 f.), and off he rides, his
next adventure being a far more courtly repetition of
the first,[26] with a greater chance of showing his knightly
prowess: there are real battles with real knights and
knightly weapons, the young lady is not won until after
Lanzelet has successfully taken on the lord's daunting
adventure, and the young lady herself is more delicate in
behaviour and sentiment. With her Lanzelet goes from
her uncle's court to her father's to be reconciled to the
family, on the way meeting and inconclusively fighting
Walwein (Gawein) whose invitation to Arthur's court he
refuses and from whom he deliberately conceals that he is
the unnamed knight Walwein has been sent to invite,
because the thought of proving his mettle against such a
renowned knight elates him. They are interrupted by a
squire with notice of a tournament and make friends,
Lanzelet eventually going to the tournament with the
young lady, Âde, and her brother. There he fights,
of course, incognito, but so distinguishes himself that
Arthur and his knights call on him and Âde in their tent,
and the unnamed knight, whose anonymity has made
him stay out of the public eye between jousts, confides
in his new friend, Walwein, his desire to complete the
quest for Plûrîs. Now things happen thick and fast.
Lanzelet falls a victim to the spell on the castle of his
foster-mother's son, seeing which Âde's brother drags
her away protesting, to be heard of no more; Lanzelet is
released by his captor to pursue a marauding neighbour,
a commission which he only undertakes when Mabûz
promises to treat his other prisoners more gently for a
year if he does; and hearing on the way that this neighbour is Iweret and that he must be defeated by the man
wishing to win his daughter, Lanzelet takes on the now

doubly-commissioned, predestined combat and thereby wins his, as one can now see, predestined bride.[27] After the battle they escape from the apprehended vengeance of Iweret's subjects and on the way they seal their union (quite informally) and are then joined by a messenger from the Fairy Queen, who must have known that Lanzelet was about to defeat Iweret for her, and the messenger tells Lanzelet who he is, who his parents are, and that his mother is Arthur's sister. Lanzelet thus joins the band of those who count Arthur their maternal uncle and who, in this poem, may include not only him and Walwein, but also Karjet (who, with Walwein, regards Lanzelet as his 'muomen sun', his maternal aunt's son) and Erec (6231, 7473). Erec's position is ambiguous: Walwein and Karjet treat him and Tristrant just as 'fellow knights' when it is a question later of releasing Lanzelet from Plûrîs, but when Erec and Walwein are handed over to the sorcerer Malduc as his fee for liberating Guinevere, because Malduc owes his father's and brother's deaths to them, both are referred to as the king's relatives. In Hartmann's *Erec*, Erec is Arthur's nephew, but not in Chrétien's, so it is perhaps less significant than one would like to think that Chrétien does not make *his* Lancelot, Guinevere's lover, Arthur's nephew either, which would have turned their relationship into a Tristan-type incest. Miss de Glinka noted[28] that from the moment of Lanzelet's becoming aware of his identity and lineage, outlandish personal names and untranslated place-names give way to more manageable personal names and translated place-names. This does not reflect the position one hundred per cent, but the change is sufficiently marked to suggest that once the hero knows where he belongs, the world becomes intelligible to him.

The Fairy Queen has marked the occasion of Lanzelet's marriage by sending him a marvellous tent, spectacularly ornamented and bearing inscriptions about the two-fold nature of love, its courage, its irrationality and its lack of moderation; the tent's ceiling is a mirror in which a lover sees his or her beloved only, whatever the distance separating them. It would seem that the tent is above all a celebration of Lanzelet and Iblis's love, rather than of Lanzelet's new-found identity, family, rank, or future power. Indeed, there is no question of Lanzelet's entering on his royal powers and duties immediately, so the tent takes account of the reality of the situation as it is at present.

Lanzelet's first thought at hearing of his kindred is to go and find his cousin Walwein, and he makes the more haste as he receives news of Queen Guinevere's having been claimed by King Valerîn on the grounds that she was allegedly betrothed to him before she was of marriageable age. Walwein cedes his right to challenge Valerîn to Lanzelet, when the latter claims Walwein's earlier promise to grant him a boon, and substantiates his equal right to defend Guinevere by breaking the news of his relationship to Arthur. The importance in Lanzelet's life of his queen cannot be better underlined than by the culmination of the quest for selfhood and knightly distinction in the predestined winning of Iblis. Guinevere is the equivalent in the Arthurian world, the queen by marriage, not by sibship. It is no accident, artistically speaking, that Lanzelet's first act after winning his own queen is to restore Arthur's queen to the Arthurian court. In the better-known Arthurian romances of the time apart from Chrétien's *Chevalier de la charrete*, the abduction and liberation of Guinevere happens off-stage; in our *Lanzelet* it is central to the theme, and happens

twice. Marie de Champagne rightly gauged the importance of Guinevere when she gave Chrétien the sensa-
tional commission to make Lancelot Guinevere's lover;
Tennyson would have maintained that she thereby sealed
the doom of the Round Table. — The battle in which
Ulrich's Lanzelet successfully challenges Valerîn's right
to Guinevere is the first battle in which the hero shows
moderation when fighting himself, and spares the van-
quished, because he was not murderous-hearted, 'wand er
niht mortgire was' (5342); and Arthur proves his chivalry,
his 'tugende stæte', and honours Lanzelet, by allowing
Valerîn to live. But Ulrich gives us a preview of the
consequences and of Valerîn's breaking of his word later.

Still Lanzelet has his own personal quest to complete,[29]
and this time his expedition to Plûrîs is successful. He
defeats the garrison, unhorsing all hundred knights who
wait there for adventurers to come along, and marries
its beautiful Queen! This is the episode which has most of
all embarrassed modern critics, and which seems to have
made Ulrich uneasy too. Ulrich may, as Miss de Glinka
and especially M. Perennec think, have a greater sense of
humour throughout than he is usually given credit for,
but one does not often sense such stark irony as in his
comment after the festivities: 'This is what the whipping
led to that Lanzelet suffered. No one can say how small a
thing may profit a man, and what is going to fall out to
his advantage or disadvantage': 'har zuo geriet der
geiselslac, / der Lanzelete wart geslagen. / ez enkan iu
nieman gesagen, / wie cleine dinc dem man gefrumet /
und was im wol ode übel kumet' (5540–4).

The Queen of Plûrîs — our fifth and last queen —
turns Lanzelet into a prisoner, depriving him of his
armour and weapons for fear of losing him, allowing
him not so much as a knife. Lanzelet's mood varies,

5

sometimes he enjoys himself, sometimes he is downcast, but always he thinks of Iblis.

Meanwhile she, at home, is undistractedly sad, and years for Lanzelet to the point of sickness. The Fairy Queen's messenger appears again, this time at Arthur's court, with a cloak as a present for the perfect lover among the ladies. The messenger embarrassingly insists on publicly interpreting the cloak's reaction to the various ladies (beginning with Guinevere) who try it on, and of course it only perfectly fits Iblis. The episode provides a theoretical survey of various faults and excesses in love, to which may be added some rather more minor episodes, and reflections interspersed by Ulrich at appropriate points in the story, together providing (like the digressions in Gottfried's *Tristan*) a broader canvas against which the love of the hero and heroine stands out. René Perennec points to the marked difference between Lanzelet's state of mind in Plûrîs and his undiluted enjoyment of his earlier amorous adventures, and sees Plûrîs and the cloak episode as counterparts of each other, highlighting the theme of marital fidelity which, in his view, is the central theme of *Lanzelet* and which could not have been brought out as it has been without the earlier adventures and this last one: in other words, Lanzelet's amorous adventures other than his relation to Iblis, far from being a source of embarrassment to the story and to his marriage, underline the uniqueness of his union with Iblis.[30] In support of this M. Perennec points out that the Fairy messenger only gives Arthur news of Lanzelet's whereabouts after Iblis has successfully tried on the cloak, so that her success in the cloak test in fact makes Lanzelet's release possible. We can also look forward and say that when Lanzelet next sets out in search of adventure deliberately, he finds it (the adventure of the princess of Thule, judge in love-cases, turned into a serpent for holding out on her lover, and only to be released by the kiss of the best knight living) — Lanzelet finds this adventure by asking Iblis, not his fellow-knights, for news of an adventure. With regard to Lanzelet's three quests, we can say that on this view, which I find an illuminating one, just as the first two quests culminate in marriage to Iblis and the gift of the love-tent, so the third turns out to be a proof of Lanzelet's inner loyalty to Iblis during separation, paralleled by Iblis's simultaneous longing for him, which, together with her implied freedom from the vices castigated by the cloak and her implied possession of the 'contrary virtues', enables her to undergo the test of the cloak successfully. M. Perennec's explanation of the celebration of marital fidelity in this and other Arthurian romances is that these reflect, unlike the earlier courtly lyric, the outlook of a society dependent on heredity for its privileges, and facing the threat of an up and coming rival class.

It is in the course of recounting the Plûrîs episode that Ulrich uses that word so often adopted by critics to characterize Lanzelet, 'der wîpsælige Lanzelet' (5529): what does not come across when it is quoted just like that is that Lanzelet's success with women is mentioned here in the ironical context: 'then the woman-lucky Lanzelet found himself obliged to marry yet again': 'dô muose aber briuten / der wîpsælige Lanzelet'. A lot of what has been said about the uncritical repetition of adventures in *Lanzelet* might have been avoided had this epithet been taken less seriously. That Lanzelet *is* successful with women, I am not denying: it begins when the ladies at the Fairy Queen's court long for him while he is still only a squire; but that Ulrich meant solemnly to present him, without any perspective, as a hero who just falls from one amorous adventure into another with no sense for anything but the enjoyment of the moment, I *would* deny.

It is in this separation from Iblis that Lanzelet is first presented as being *trûric* (5645). Yet he had grown up in a palace which had the property of making happy for life anyone who spent as much as a day there: 'die steine heten sölhe kraft, / die an daz hûs wârn geleit, / daz man uns dervon seit, / swer dâ wonet einen tac, / daz er niemer riuwe pflac / und imer vrœlîche warp / unz an die stunt daz er erstarp' (234–40). Lanzelet's grieving for Iblis is not a slip of Ulrich's pen. When he and the four knights who rescue him reach Arthur, who they have heard has been wounded in the pursuit of the perjured and treacherous Valerîn, who has abducted Guinevere, they weep bitterly (6848 f.); it would have been wolfish to avoid *trûren*, Ulrich says (6853 f.). The cause of their *trûren* is that Arthur has renounced *fröide* (6871), which means that the court from whose festival Iblis held back while she alone was mourning has lost its raison d'être:[31] the enhancement of life that the court should represent, in Medieval eyes, has become impossible. And why? *Because the Queen is lost.* It is for Queen Guinevere that Erec and Walwein are willing to be surrendered to their mortal enemy the sorcerer, and it is Lanzelet who can assure Arthur that they will, without having to ask them first; he infers it from their previous devotion to Arthur and from knowledge of what his own response would be to such a request. Lanzelet emerges as the wise counsellor in this episode,[32] showing his sympathy with Arthur by his own grief but curbing that of Arthur's son, Lôût, with the prospect of loyal support and a reminder of the need for some plan to circumvent the impregnability of Valerîn's castle (a plan eventually thought up by Tristrant), and knowing exactly what can be demanded of the solidarity of Arthur's knights and not being afraid to act on that knowledge or allowing himself to be restricted by protocol to asking Erec and Walwein first. Lanzelet seems to be gaining in emotional depth *and* in maturity of judgement.

On Guinevere's release, the court returns to a muted *vröide*, muted by the loss of Erec and Walwein. But neither Iblis nor anything else can console Lanzelet — and here he is mentioned individually and alone — for the thought of what Erec and Walwein are undergoing and the certain prospect of their death: 'Lanzelet dô niht enlie / durch wîp noch durch ander guot, / im wære *trûric* der muot' (7480–2): again, and this time specifically of Lanzelet, *trûren*. Only initially can it be said of Lanzelet, 'er enweiz niht waz trûren ist' (1341). Lanzelet's successful rescue of Erec and Walwein is the crowning event in the series of episodes successively showing Lanzelet, in feelings and in action, as a true husband, a true subject, and a true member of the knightly fraternity. The seal is set on his proving of himself by his release of the bewitched Princess of Thule, which shows him to be by definition the best knight living.[33]

The double coronation of Lanzelet, first in his own country and then in Iblis's, takes up more space in Ulrich's narrative than even the episodes of Iweret and the fairy queen's tent combined, which were together over 1,000 lines long, out of the 9,000+ of the poem. Ulrich lays himself out to communicate the magnificence of these coronation feasts, at which Arthur is in his turn a guest, and recounts the preliminary negotiations in detail, especially the formal acceptance of Lanzelet by his father's subjects, who encourage him to treat them more

kindly than his father had. Undoubtedly M. Perennec is
right in pointing to Ulrich's repeated insistence at all
levels of overlordship on the evils of tyranny, of power
without consideration for the rights of those less elevated,
and in seeing in the poem of *Lanzelet* among other things
a speculum as it were of the ideal Medieval king's relationship with his vassals.[34] Iblis, too, uses her influence only
in the service of what is worthy, so Ulrich says: 'diu riet
im niht wan êre' (9387), and M. Perennec points to a
similar moral twist given by Hartmann to the concluding
lines of *Erec*. Dynastic considerations are not forgotten in
Lanzelet: Lanzelet and Iblis have four children, three sons
and a daughter, just enough, as Ulrich points out (9379),
for Iweret's three kingdoms and Lanzelet's one (it would
seem that Lanzelet, true to Ulrich's ideal, relinquishes the
kingdoms Iweret had conquered by force, unless they
have seceded meanwhile). What is interesting is that
Lanzelet appears to settle in Iweret's kingdom — in other
words, 'er heiratet ein'. Presumably he could rely on his
own kinsmen at home, one of whom at least has proved
faithful, to rule Genewîs for him, but had to see to
Iweret's kingdom himself. But it enhances yet more the
importance of his queen that he should live in *her* kingdom. He won her in the middle of the book, finding her
destined for him as he fulfilled the task imposed by the
queen who fostered him for his own mother, chance and
destiny thus working hand-in-hand; his first act was to
rescue Arthur's queen; and after his and Iblis's loyalty
to one another has been demonstrated and Guinevere
again rescued, this time at a price that Arthur himself
feels unable to ask of his knights, but for the fact that they
volunteer, Lanzelet and Iblis embark on a model reign
in which love and kingship seem inseparable, and which
appropriately *ends* undividedly too, in that they both die

on the same day. They seem to have no further need for their tent, which they give to Guinevere. Iblis would have given her cloak, in which she is crowned, to Keiîn's mistress, but for its peculiar behaviour on that lady. The intensification of Ulrich's references to Lanzelet's *sælde* in this final section shows that Lanzelet has reached the state of being the ideal king, *sælde* indicating a kind of secular charisma in the context of kingship. The most striking references to the constancy of his *sælde* come much earlier: Lady Sælde had pledged herself to be a permanent member of his household (1582 f.), he was born *sælic* (2756), but the reality comes above all in achieving, not some special feat or insight, but the adequate filling of his own station in life, to which he had been born. The wheel has come full circle, and so the mountain has apparently brought forth a mouse — only every mouse, taken seriously, has turned out to be a mountain.

REFERENCES

[1] Ulrich von Zatzikhoven, *Lanzelet*, ed. K. A. Hahn, Frankfurt am Main, 1845, repr. de Gruyter (Berlin, 1965).

[2] Armgart Trendelenburg, *Aufbau und Funktion der Motive im Lanzelet Ulrichs von Zatzikhoven im Vergleich mit den deutschen Artusromanen um 1200*, Diss. phil. (Tübingen, 1955).

Teresa Mary de Glinka-Janczewski, *Ulrich von Zatzikhoven's 'Lanzelet': a critical study*, M.A. thesis (London, 1963).

René Perennec, *Ulrich von Zatzikhoven, Lanzelet*, diss. (Paris, 1970–1).

[3] Chrétien de Troyes, *Le Chevalier de la charrete*, ed. Mario Roques (Paris, 1958).

[4] Eugène Vinaver, *Form and Meaning in Medieval Romance*, MHRA (Cambridge, 1967).

[5] Ingeborg Schröbler, *Von den Grenzen des Verstehens mittelalterlicher Dichtung*, *GRM*, 44 (1963), 1–14.

[6] Gustav Ehrismann, *Geschichte der deutschen Literatur biz zum Ausgang des Mittelalters*, Pt. 2,2,2 (Schlußband) (Munich, 1935), p. 6.

[7] Helmut de Boor, *Die höfische Literatur*, 4th ed. (de Boor–Newald, Geschichte der deutschen Literatur, Vol. 2), p. 86.

[8] Teresa de Glinka-Janczewski, op. cit., p. 103.

[9] Walther Joh. Schröder, *Spielmannsepik* (Sammlung Metzler, 19), (Stuttgart, 1962).

[10] Luise Lerner, *Studien zur Komposition des höfischen Romans im 13. Jahrhundert* (Münster, 1936) (Forschungen zur deutschen Sprache und Dichtung, 7), pp. 17–20, contrasting the German courtly romance with pre-courtly narrative

poetry, stresses the structural *similarities* between *Lanzelet* and Hartmann's *Iwein* and Wolfram's *Parzival*.

[11] Chrétien de Troyes, *Erec et Enide*, ed. Mario Roques (Paris, 1965).

[12] Chrétien de Troyes, *Le Chevalier au lion*, ed. Mario Roques (Paris, 1963).

[13] Luise Lerner's different perspective would at least at first sight lead to a questioning of this concept, see her assessment of Wolfram's *Parzival*, op. cit., pp. 10–14.

[14] This assumption is also questioned by Armgart Trendelenburg, op. cit., p. 9.

[15] J.-P. Collas, *The Romantic Hero of the Twelfth Century*, in: Medieval Miscellany presented to Eugène Vinaver (Manchester U.P., 1965), pp. 80–96.

[16] Compare Hugo Kuhn, *Die Klassik des Rittertums in der Stauferzeit*, Annalen der deutschen Literatur (Stuttgart, 1952), p. 135 f.: '... ein in drei Stufen aufsteigender Minneweg ... verschlingt sich mit den drei Stufen seines Ritterwegs zur Tafelrunde: Einladung, Turnier, Bewährungskampf gegen die Räuber der Ginover.'

[17] In a talk to the London Medieval Society on 29 October 1969, entitled 'The Ethos of Arthurian Chivalry'. Compare *The Problems of a New Edition of Ulrich von Zatzikhoven's 'Lanzelet'*, in: Probleme mittelalterlicher Überlieferung und Textkritik, ed. P. F. Ganz and W. Schröder (Berlin, 1968), p. 79.

[18] On the grading of the ladies see also Luise Lerner, op. cit., p. 18, and Armgart Trendelenburg, op. cit., pp. 22–4.

[19] Franz Beyerle, *Der 'Arme Heinrich' Hartmanns von Aue als Zeugnis mittelalterlichen Ständewesens*, Fs. Hans Fehr (Arbeiten zur Rechtssoziologie und Rechtsgeschichte 1) (Karlsruhe, 1948), 27–46.

[20] Hermann Conrad, *Deutsche Rechtsgeschichte*, Vol. 1 (Karlsruhe, 1954), p. 396.

[21] Ibid., pp. 398–402.

[22] Gerta Telger, *Die altfranzösische Gregoriuslegende* (Arbeiten zur Romanischen Philologie, 5) (Münster, 1933).

[23] For a treatment of original sin in an exposition of the *Song of Songs* see Bede, MPL 91,1070.

[24] See also Uwe Ruberg, *Die Suche im Prosa-Lancelot*, ZfdA, 92 (1963–4), esp. pp. 124–7.

[25] Walter Ohly, *Die heilsgeschichtliche Struktur der Epen Hartmanns von Aue*, Diss. phil. (F.U. Berlin, 1958), pp. 23 ff.

[26] On gradation in Lanzelet's adventures, see Luise Lerner, op. cit., p. 18, and Armgart Trendelenburg, op. cit., p. 13.

[27] On predestination in *Lanzelet* see also Armgart Trendelenburg, op. cit., passim.

[28] Op. cit., p. 136 f.

[29] On the function of this episode as a link between past and future, and in destroying Lanzelet and Iblis's 'Freude', see Armgart Trendelenburg, op. cit., pp. 28 f.

[30] Compare also Luise Lerner, op. cit., p. 18, and Armgart Trendelenburg, op. cit., pp. 25–30.

[31] Compare T. A. Shippey, *The Uses of Chivalry: 'Erec' and 'Gawain'*, MLR, 66 (1971), 241–50.

[32] Teresa de Glinka-Janczewski, op. cit., p. 104.

[33] Luise Lerner, op. cit., p. 19.

[34] Luise Lerner's title to her second main division, 'Erziehung zum Landesherrn 4958 ff.', op. cit., p. 17, is not really substantiated on pp. 18–20.

The Path of Life

Attitudes to the Bible in some autobiographies of the seventeenth and eighteenth centuries

By Derek Bowman

A LMOST inevitably all of us here have been bereaved in our time. Here is how a woman of the seventeenth century, Elizabeth Avery, faces the death of a dear child of hers:

... I had great afflictions, and amongst others, by the loss of my children, God's rod was laid heavy upon me, insomuch, That he struck three of them together; and one childe above all, a most sweet childe, and one, that I least thought of them all would have died, was very ill; and we were talking (I, my Husband, and some Friends,) together of comfortable things, and amongst others of David, when he said of his childe (dead) I shall go to it, it shall not return to me. Ay sayes one, that is to the grave; which word wounded me; and I went into the Garden to wail and moan my self; but soon after, my Husband came and told me my childe was dying; at which I was left in an horror, as if I were in Hell, none could comfort me, nothing could satisfie me, no Friends, nothing; then it was sad indeed to me, a Hell indeed. I sent for the Doctor and others, but to no purpose. Yet after this the Lord wrought on me much; and one, a Minister of Christ, that had power from God to do me good, gave me much satisfaction by a Letter of his: And after that, me thoughts, I was content to part with all, and to let all go; then God tryed me, and took away another childe from me, and I could bear it very well, and was not troubled, but rather did rejoyce within me to be thus tryed ...[1]

Elizabeth Avery, her husband and her friends, members of John Rogers's Independent congregation in Dublin in 1653, associate their affliction with that of David, as recounted in chapter twelve of the Second Book of Samuel. King David committed adultery with Bathsheba, the wife of Uriah the Hittite, whom David then got killed by sending him into battle where the fighting was thickest. The child born of David's sin is struck down by the Lord. David fasts and grieves for the sick child, as long as it is alive, but on learning of its death, he washes, puts on fresh clothing, worships in the temple, then has a meal, ready to face life again. When he is reproached with callousness he answers:

While the child was yet alive, I fasted and wept: for I said, Who can tell whether God will be gracious to me, that the child may live?

But now he is dead, wherefore should I fast? can I bring him back again? I shall go to him, but he shall not return to me.[2]

It is clear from the many autobiographies, sometimes short, sometimes long, of Elizabeth Avery and her like that the stories of the Bible, being the Word of God, had tremendous power. They struck home, intensifying, deepening the joys and sorrows of people's lives. What happened to ordinary folk like themselves had also happened to the patriarchs, to God's people, to Christ Himself — we have this on the highest authority. This awareness spelt no easy consolation — though it is undoubtedly a comfort to know that others, and especially our Creator and Saviour, have experienced similar trials to one's own — indeed, as in Elizabeth Avery's case, the reading or hearing of a similar incident in the Bible to an experience the recipient was undergoing could be very painful. Eventually, however, by articulating that person's overwhelming feelings in terms of the Scripture, often with the support of a Minister of the Gospel, it set them in the right perspective. Pondering on the Bible thereby clothed the events of this life, however distressing, in a literate dignity hallowed by the timeless Church. Human experience, seen in the light of eternity, was changed from confusion into mystery, for does not God's Providence underlie everything that happens to us in this sublunary world? — In John Bunyan's staunch words: 'to live upon God that is invisible',[3] that is the way not to faint. So, aided by the bible-story, sustained by her minister, Elizabeth Avery — and how many others before and after! — learns patience under her sufferings. A century later in Switzerland the yarn-merchant Ulrich Bräker was, in his own special fashion, to use the very same story of David, when writing of the loss of two of his children in the great plague of 1772.[4] The Bible, then, got people to face facts, a very necessary accomplishment in this life.

Facing facts. In this paper I wish to show a little of how our forebears used the Bible to this end. First I shall enlarge on the consolations — 'comfortable things' — that men and women obtained from the Scriptures. Then I shall treat the related question of exemplars of the Old and New Testaments, the figures that Christians used to fortify or discipline themselves, even to the point of mystical identification. Next I shall discuss the mysterious part played by imagery in the Bible and in people's minds. Finally I shall contrast the drastic strenuousness of the Puritan and Pietist attitude to life, so much shaped by the Bible, with a new irony, that, during the course of the eighteenth century, came on to the scene.

Since the Fall, the world has by all accounts always been in a bad way; certainly the autobiographers of the seventeenth and eighteenth centuries whom I have chosen to depict had a hard time of it. Conditions were harsh then: leaving material hardships aside, infant mortality and sickness, which could easily take a dangerous turn, were familiar to every household. Thus Hemme Hayen, a Frisian farmer, apparently of some standing, in the course of recounting his life to some friends in 1689, remarks quite incidentally:

In den 23. Jahren/ die ich mit meiner Frau gelebet/ haben wir 12. Kinder gehabt; doch niemals mehr als 3. beysammen im Leben: und die letzt=übergebliebene seynd gewesen/ unsere erstgebohrne Tochter Esse, und zwey Söhne/ Haye und Lambert.[5]

Not that people always took their ills lying down, so to speak. — Hemme Hayen again:

Es bekam auch meine Frau von dem Kinder=Zeugen viele Jahr lang eine ungemeine Pein durch alle ihre Glieder/ welche je länger je ärger wurde/ man mochte auch Mittel brauchen welche man wolte. Bey allen diesen Leibes=Schwachheiten/ die auch unsere Nachbaren zum Mitleiden erweckten/ trug sichs offtmals zu/ daß meine Hausfrau/ als ihr Hertz von Leiden überlieff/ zu mir sagte: Mein lieber Mann! wie solls noch endlich mit uns gehen? Wann uns der HErr aller unserer Güter beraubt/ was sollen wir dann endlich anfangen? Worauf ich antwortete: Kind/ sey doch nur wol zu frieden! GOtt wird alles machen nach seinem Belieben/ so wie es am besten ist . . . Ich stellete ihr einsmals das Exempel Hiobs und all sein Leiden vor; worauff sie mit solcher Bangigkeit/ als sie konte/ antwortete: Das Leiden Hiobs war nimmermehr so langwierig! Es war wol überaus groß; allein es hörete wieder auf/ und er bekam darnach mehr/ als er zuvor gehabt hatte: Allein unser Leiden hat kein Ende/ es drücket immer härter und härter/ und bleibt beständig bey uns.[6]

Here we see an old couple, sitting by the fire (so often mentioned in older autobiographies), talking over their

troubles which are harrowing enough, trying to draw
what strength they can from their faith. It is not easy.
Versed in the Scriptures, familiar since childhood with its
heroes, they argue over one of its great figures, Job,
seeing their trials in the light of his, comparing and
contrasting their lot with his, struggling to *understand*.
What else can they do? I believe it was Pavese who once
said: true reading and writing are products of human
need. To search the Scriptures and wrestle with them,
bringing their lives to bear on them, sizing up what they
read and eliciting its meaning as fully as they can in the
light of their own unique experience — this is how in
those days Hemme Hayen and his ailing wife, and
countless others, kept going. To do so may not have
taken the actual pain away, but it did give it dignity: it
helped the sufferer to grit his teeth and bear his lot.[7] But
there *was* hope. Heaven was to come; there were even
glimpses of it here — and look what happened to Job
in the end! As John Bunyan puts it: 'My dear Children,
The Milk and Honey is beyond this Wilderness'.[8] Hemme
Hayen goes on — and through the snatches of dialogue
one can almost hear his anxious wife worriting him:

Als sie biszweilen bekümmert war/ ich mögte vor ihr sterben;
[a very real dread in those days] tröstete ich sie mit dem Exempel
der armen Wittib/ die durch Elisa auf GOttes Befehl Hülff
bekam. Ja/ dachte sie/ GOtt hat das damals wol gethan; allein
solte er das wol nun auch an uns beweisen? Ich aber sagte zu
ihr: Ja/ GOtt ist jetztund eben so mächtig/ als damals! Also
begab sie sich hierin zu frieden.[9]

For how long? one wonders. All the more need, then,
for the constant comfort of the Word. But it was undoubtedly consoling to Hemme Hayen and his wife to
know that ultimately the God of Abraham and Isaac is

still the same God, omnipotent, tender-hearted as ever.
What He has done through Elisha to help the poor
woman, and so many distressed souls besides, in the Bible
and out, He will do for them too. Why! God seems to
have gone out of his way to help the barren and the
needy: as Hannah and later Mary sing:

> He hath put down the mighty from their seats,
> and exalted them of low degree.
> He hath filled the hungry with good things; and
> the rich he hath sent empty away.[10]

Only trust. Meditation on the Bible inculcated trust in the
heart of the believer. He was not alone. Suffering was not
futile, life meaningless. Surely this is the most important
sense of all for a mortal to have.

How is this seen in John Bunyan's case? A lively
sense of God's grace effected in Christ's one oblation of
Himself once offered came to equip Bunyan to meet any
trial that might await him. Such fortitude, as I shall show,
was hard-won, since Bunyan was clearly a most sensitive,
not to say scrupulous, man. Thus, writing in *Grace
Abounding to the Chief of Sinners*, of his separation from his
family, while incarcerated for his preaching, he describes
his feelings in that intensely physical way he has, born of a
mind fed on the imagery of the Bible, where the spiritual
realm is clothed in physical garb: '. . . the parting with
my Wife and poor Children hath oft been to me in this
place as the pulling the flesh from my bones . . .'.[11] He
bewails the fate especially of his poor blind child left
behind, then putting himself in the position he was,
when he had to go, he shows how he bore up:

. . . but yet recalling my self, thought I, I must venture you all
with God, though it goeth to the quick to leave you. O I saw
in this condition I was as a man who was pulling down his

house upon the head of his Wife and Children; yet thought I,
I must do it, I must do it.[12]

One of Bunyan's great strengths is rhythmically, physically to convey in the very style the to-and fro-ing of his
mind and heart. In this, his physicality, he recalls an
earlier stage of Christianity. So we catch him just as the
thought of a rather minor Old Testament incident
stiffens his resolve—but perhaps it is wrong thus to speak
of 'minor', since any biblical incident, any experience
could be of the utmost significance to the believer: 'and
now I thought of those two milch Kine that were to carry
the Ark of God into another Country, and to leave their
Calves behind them, 1 Sam. VI. 10, 11, 12.'[13] The unsearch-
able riches of the Bible yielded treasures new and old,
fitting every situation in life. They underpinned the
Puritan's life, endowing human experience with religious
significance, poetry, the profoundest meaning, as Hamann
was to realize: 'Die Poeterey, sagt Martin Opitz, ist
anfangs nichts anders als eine verborgene Theologie und
Unterricht von göttlichen Sachen gewesen.'[14]

In those Puritan times, then, the reading of the Bible
was always directed towards intensifying the spiritual
life of the individual. The Word is to dwell richly in him:
exegesis is directed towards this end — in a phrase of
the time, 'walke the word aright, as well as divide the
word aright'.[15] Preachers saw to this in every sermon
they preached, awakening or opening the Bible to their
flock. Tyndale exhorts his readers to take 'the stories
and lives which are contained in the Bible for sure and
undoubted examples that God will so deal with us unto
the world's end.'[16]

I have been speaking of the milk of the Word; the
Bible in St Paul's words could also be 'sharper than any
two-edged sword, piercing even to the dividing asunder

of soul and spirit, and of the joints and marrow, and is a discerner of the thoughts and intents of the heart'.[17] John Bunyan, in his self-torturing fashion, sees himself as one after another of its many villains. Now he is the adulterer who shall die, spoken of in Deuteronomy XXII. 25, now Cain, the marked fratricide doomed to wander the earth (as Hamann was also to see himself), now David in his sins, now, for years of torment, that Esau, depicted by St Paul:

who for one morsel of meat sold his Birth-right; for ye know how that afterwards when he would have inherited the blessing, he was rejected, for he found no place of repentance, though he sought it carefully with tears, Heb. XII. 16, 17.[18]

When, only after terrible struggles, Bunyan finally consents to Satan's urgings to sell Christ, 'Sell him, sell him, sell him, sell him',[19] he well nigh despairs. Now he is not even Peter: *he* only denied his master, while he had sold his Saviour: 'Wherefore' he writes, 'I thought with my self, that I came nearer to Judas, than either to David or Peter',[20] that Judas, who, falling headlong, burst asunder, and all his bowels gushed out.[21] The most horrible awareness Bunyan has is that he has been, like Esau, rejected, rejected utterly and for all eternity. Nothing he can do can help. Only when, after years of turmoil, he realizes that he is justified freely by God's grace through the redemption that is in Christ Jesus, is the problem of his life resolved. Now he is an Heir of God. He sees more in these words, 'Heirs of God!' than ever he can express as long as he lives.[22] Hamann was to go through a similar ordeal, as I shall try to show later.

Bunyan's is the hard Protestant Puritanical way, a constant warring against the promptings of Satan. I now wish to touch on another process, the age-old

Catholic way of the mystic — Mary as opposed to Martha.
The mystic conceives of the indwelling Christ and fosters
in his soul the incidents of Christ's birth, life, passion,
death and resurrection. This is the way traced by Hemme
Hayen, whom we have already seen consoling his wife
in their troubles. It is to be found in Reitz's *Historie der
Wiedergebohrenen*, published at Itzstein in 1717, a massive
popular edifying work of the time, a book, incidentally,
full of accounts of seventeenth-century British Puritans.

Hayen seems to have been influenced in his quest, if
one may term it such, first and foremost by the Bible,
which he says, his mother liked to see him reading, but
also by the *Schatz der Seelen* and the *Nachfolge Christi von
Kempis*, and Jacob Böhme's *Der Weg zu Christo*. Although
Hayen had not, before his illumination, actually read
Böhme, the local preacher, Benjamin Potinius of Marien-
hoven, had six months before spoken of Böhme's lofty
mystical experience.

After various trials, and after due preparation for the
celebration of Easter by reading Isaiah chapters fifty-five
to sixty-one inclusive, Hayen experiences his illumination, his 'Erleuchtung' (as he calls it). This leads to the
climax of his brief 'life-story', an account of his physical
enacting of the Passion of Christ, during which Hayen
receives the stigmata:

Hierauff zeigete sich nun das Leiden des Herrn Jesu von Anfang
bisz zum Ende/ dergestalt/ daß ich auch selbst äusserlich
mit meinen Armen und Händen als entbunden zu werden mich
mußte schicken und anstellen. Und als der Tod von dem
Herrn Jesu in mir solte gehalten werden/ dieweil meine Arme
und Hände auszwendig also auszgestrecket waren/ fühlete ich
in der That und wesentlich eine Pein/ die unauszsprechlich war.
Mein Sohn Haye ließ auff die Zeit eine steinerne Schüssel aus
seiner Hand in Stücken fallen: und mit dem Fall war es nicht

6

anders/ als ob ich natürlicher weise und empfindlich mit einem Schwerdt durchstochen und getödtet würde; so daß mir der nasse Schweiß ausz dem Angesicht ausbrach.[23]

He goes on to say that he got and still bears in his right hand a mark of the cross, which marks are rare. Later Hayen goes to bed and rests for forty hours before rising. He observes that these forty hours signify the burial of the Lord Jesus Christ who lay forty hours in the grave before He rose, just as Adam slept that number of hours before he got Eve. Here one can see how much Hayen still moves in the age-old timeless world of Christian typology, that world which, with the rise of the 'Auf-klärung', was to fade with such tragic rapidity in people's minds, though Hamann did stand out against this baleful development, a Daniel here as in so many of his con-victions.

Before he gets up, Hayen looks to the foot of his bed and there leaning against the wall by the bedroom door stands Aaron's rod — the spirit tells him so — and as he watches it, it grows green, blossoms and bears almonds. The almond-tree, 'Mandelbaum', is so distinct that, even though Hayen has, as he says, never actually seen one, the local preacher, three days after, when Hayen visits him, recognizes it as such right away from his description.

May I now dwell on this image of the almond-tree for a moment, since, in my view, it provides a clear example of the way in those days the minds and hearts of men and women were peopled with the imagery, the whole figurative wealth of the Scriptures, whose rich, exotic, exuberant, startling, middle-east features — the bearers of 'sparkles' or 'glancings' or 'bright gleamings' in the language of the time — strangely contrasted and yet mingled with the phenomena of nature all around.

There in misty seventeenth-century West Friesland on a farmstead near the village of Opgant a visionary farmer sees an almond-tree blossom by his bedroom-wall, something he has never actually found growing. So implanted, however, is it in his imagination by close readings of the Bible and devotional literature — I think of the intentness manifest in Rembrandt's etching of a girl reading — so inculcated by sermons from and conversations with preachers and sectaries, reinforced perhaps by the study of pictorial representations on triptychs or in breviaries and bibles such as the 'Armenbibel', which shows on one page three biblical scenes — the first, God's appearing to Moses in the burning bush, the second, the greening of Aaron's rod, and the third, Christ's nativity[24] — that Hemme Hayen immediately recognizes the almond-tree as Aaron's rod: 'der Geist sagte mir/ daß es die wäre.'[25] A hallucination? Such a charge is too cheap, too dismissive. What is required of literary criticism, as indeed of any descriptive language, is that it should do justice to its subject-matter, however strange: as Goethe puts it: 'Die Gewalt einer Sprache ist nicht, daß sie das Fremde abweist, sondern daß sie es verschlingt.'[26] The important thing about the almond-tree for Hayen and his like was that it was not just a vision, nor just a plant, but a symbol, a figure of Christ Himself. Its beauty like that of nature, like the course of a human life, like history, lies in its infinite eternal meaning, which meaning is to be found in the Bible, the Word. As Hamann was to put it in the third of his fragments, 'Brocken', of 1758:

Natur und Geschichte sind ... die zwey großen *Commentarii* des Göttlichen Worts, und dieses hingegen der einzige Schlüssel, uns eine Erkenntniß in beiden zu eröffnen.[27]

And so the quintessence of Hayen's whole life is distilled in those mystical experiences of his, his treasures.

Language in these old spiritual autobiographies is accordingly immensely poetic, heaven and earth and hell being close at hand, solid, palpable, 'in der Tat und wesentlich'.[28] Take such a sentence from John Bunyan's *Grace Abounding* as:

At which time, my Understanding was so enlightened, that I was as though I had seen the Lord Jesus look down from Heaven through the Tiles upon me, and direct these words unto me.[29]

Through the Tiles. The dimensions in which men lived seem to have been very different from ours, so much vaster, even though (or perhaps because?) people did not move about then as much as we do. St Augustine's words are still apt:

... men go out and gaze in astonishment at high mountains, the huge waves of the sea, the broad reaches of rivers, the ocean that encircles the world, or the stars in their courses. But they pay no attention to themselves.[30]

The spiritual and the material, then, can and do coalesce for man, but only, preachers reiterate, when man's heart is awakened, when the Bible is opened or discovered, for: '... the natural man', St Paul warns, 'receiveth not the things of the Spirit of God ... because they are spiritually discerned',[31] or, in Anna Trapnel's words: '... they only that have the language of *Canaan* shall be taken into thy *Canaan*, and shall have the honey drops there'.[32] It is the constant burden of seventeenth-century spiritual autobiographers that the meaning of St Paul's Epistles only dawns on the Christian at a late stage in his progress. Only then will the benighted sinner who has too long laboured in Egypt, cross the Red Sea, Pharoah's chariots drowning after him, eventually to enter the Promised Land; only then will Babylon fall in the heart and resplendent New Jerusalem, the Heavenly City rear up. The traditional images from the Pentateuch and The Revelation of St John are met with again and again, undergoing endless variations, according to the auto-biographers' unique personalities and lives. London merges with Nineveh; Palestine and Bunyan's Bedford-shire illuminate each other in the light of God's own presence:

'Have you never a Hill Mizar to remember?' he writes. 'Have you forgot the Close, the Milk-house, the Stable, the Barn, and the like, where God did visit your Soul?'[33]

The pity is that such spiritualizing of the material could become in the hands of some writers of the later seven-teenth century an early, hard-headed, capitalist device for getting more out of workers. Here is an example, from the Revd John Collinges's *The Weaver's Pocket-Book or, Weaving Spiritualized*:

... my self have known many who came to considerable estates, who have told me they begun with ten pound; they passed but with a staff over *Jordan*, and at their coming back had great droves.[34]

To spiritualize every object, by drawing glib biblical parallels, could become a moralizing ritual, as one sees here in John Collinges's manual or in John Flavel's *Naviga-tion Spiritualiz'd or, a New Compass for Seamen* of 1698; the latter in his 'Epistle Dedicatory' praises real sailors who 'drive a Trade for Heaven, and are diligent to secure the happiness of their Immortal souls, in the Insurance-Office above'![35]

But to return to the language of Canaan. How does such imagery work? Here one can only hint at a mystery. Bunyan's *Grace Abounding* is a case in point. Never out of the Bible, as he says, he is so susceptible to its impact that

its words have a physical effect on him: a scripture seizes
upon his soul, a word takes hold of him, Scriptures meet
in his heart, a sentence bolts in upon him; 'O this word
"For the Scripture cannot be broken" would rend the
caul of my heart' [a reference to Hosea XIII. 8].[36] The
thought torments Bunyan that he should say of Christ
'Let him go if he will':

In struggling to resist this wickedness my very Body also
would be put into action or motion, by way of pushing or
thrusting with my hands or elbows.[37]

A born poet, Burnyan is obsessed with the body, with
the concrete, and feels its presence and its power in all
experience, using it passionately to express his searing
spiritual awareness. In this connexion Giambattista Vico
in his *New Science* of 1744, posing the problem philosophically and linguistically in the modern fashion, comments:

The human mind is naturally inclined by the senses to see
itself externally in the body, and only with great difficulty does
it come to attend to itself by means of reflection.
This axiom gives us the universal principle of etymology in
all languages: words are carried over from bodies and from the
properties of bodies to express the things of the mind.[38]

This process is one of the incalculable benefits of the
Bible, indeed of Christ Himself Who used everything,
even his own spittle, to show the divine power and
meaning fulfilling all creation, to show us ourselves.
The Church Militant, the saints carry on this process of
mystical analogy: 'Thy will be done in earth as it is in
heaven.' Thus Frater Thomas de Celano writes of St
Francis of Assisi: 'De toto corpore fecerat linguam'[39] —
of his whole body he had made a tongue, a language.
Hamann, profound Christian that he is, sees the process
theologically instead of philosophically, as Vico does.

Hamann was full of the sense that God needed parables in order to speak with men, since all our knowledge comes through the senses and through figures: he writes in his first letter to Lavater on 17 January 1778:

Ihnen von Grund meiner Seele zu sagen, ist mein ganzes Christenthum (ich mag zu den fetten oder magern Kühen Pharaons gehören) ein Geschmack an *Zeichen*, und an den Elementen des Wassers, des Brods, des Weins.[40]

He is like St Augustine in this, when the saint writes:

The presentation of truth through signs has great power to feed and fan that ardent love, by which, as under some law of gravitation, we flicker upwards, or inwards, to our place of rest.[41]

It is now time to concentrate on Hamann. His conception of signs springs from his experience of God's Word speaking to him through the Bible, and his whole life was, after his conversion, devoted to enlarging and deepening this, his sacramental view, to include all the phenomena of life. Like St Paul, he sees God revealing Himself to us in things beneath Him, indeed going out of His way to choose whatever is smallest, most despised — the infinite condescension of God to man as seen in the Incarnation, when His Son came to visit us in great humility. In a sublime letter to G. E. Lindner, dated 3 August 1759, Hamann realizes how something of this humbling process takes place in every one of us in the very act of speech — the most human thing we have, Fontane called language — as the spiritual thoughts of our souls take on flesh in the shape of sounds, of language.[42] God's emptying of Himself to man, to His creation, culminating in the Crucifixion, can hardly be touched by our finite, creaturely minds, never mind grasped or expressed anywhere near adequately. How can we, His creatures, perceive the mystery of our being? Only in reverence, trust, humility. 'Gedanken über meinen Lebenslauf' is Hamann's approach at an answer.

In this short but infinitely profound autobiography Hamann shows how, like Jabez, a child of sorrow, he has to go through the hell of self-knowledge, before he comes to see the meaning of the Bible, the claims which God has on each sinful soul, and his own in particular: '... nichts als die Höllenfahrt der Selbsterkenntnis bahnt uns den Weg zur Vergötterung.'[43] Spiritually and materially at the end of his tether in London in the spring of 1758, Hamann turns to the Bible as his only hope, and reads it through, concentrating on every word. As he reads, certain things emerge: above all, God would not let His people go, however much they erred. In a turmoil, the children of Israel would ask what He wanted of them, then they would repent, then promptly forget their repentance and sin anew, but then at last, realizing their own utter powerlessness, they pleaded for a redeemer:

... nichts als einen Erlöser, einen Fürsprecher, einen Mittler anriefen, ohne den sie unmöglich Gott weder recht fürchten, noch recht lieben konnten.[44]

These observations of his seem very mysterious to him. On the evening of 31 March he reads the fifth chapter of Deuteronomy. The experience overwhelms him. He falls into deep contemplation; Abel haunts his mind, that Abel of whom God said: '[the earth] hath opened her mouth to receive thy brother's blood from thy hand'[45] (here Hamann transposes the figures of Cain and Abel). He feels his heart thump, he hears a voice from the depths sigh and groan, the voice of blood, of a slain brother demanding revenge, should he continue to stop his ears against it. It was his own deafness that had made

Cain to wander the earth, a criminal: 'daß eben dieß
Kain unstätig und flüchtig machte.'[46] Then he feels his
heart suddenly dilate. It bursts into tears. No longer can
he hold it back. *He* is the fratricide: '. . . ich der Brudermörder, der Brudermörder seines eingebornen Sohnes.'[47]
Now he recognizes his sins in the story of the Jewish
people. The breakthrough has come, as (in Hamann's
words) God's spirit reveals more and more the mystery
of divine love and the benefit of faith in our gracious and
only Saviour. This is conversion. The whole direction
of Hamann's life is changed. He has come to feel the
truth that the Psalmist expressed centuries before: 'Thou
wilt show me the path of life: in thy presence is fulness of
joy; at thy right hand there are pleasures for evermore.'[48]

Now in my final section I wish to show a new mood
coming over autobiographers of the later eighteenth
century. Enough has been said to indicate the deadly
seriousness of the Puritan and Pietist attitude to life.
Bunyan expresses it in the Preface to *Grace Abounding* in
unforgettable words:

God did not play in convincing of me; the Devil did not play
in tempting of me; neither did I play when I sunk as into a
bottomless pit, when the pangs of hell caught hold upon me:
wherefore I may not play in my relating of them, but be plain
and simple, and lay down the thing as it was.[49]

The thing as it was. Now listen to Ulrich Bräker, the
author of the symptomatically entitled *Lebensgeschichte und
Natürliche Ebentheuer des Armen Mannes im Tockenburg*,[50]
published in 1789, as he discusses his motive for writing:

Obschon ich die Vorreden sonst hasse, muß ich doch ein
Wörtchen zum voraus sagen, ehe ich diese Blätter, weiß noch
selbst nicht mit was vor Zeug überschmiere. Was mich dazu
bewogen? Eitelkeit? — Freylich! — Einmal ist die Schreib-
sucht da, etc.[51]

What a difference in tone! Depicting his restless youth, Bräker compares himself to Cain, a stock biblical figure (as we have seen), but again how different the tone is from that of Bunyan or Hamann:

Nun von jenem Zeitpunkt an war ich unstät und flüchtig, wie Cain. Bald bestuhnd meine Arbeit im Taglöhnen; bald zügelte ich für meinen Vater das Salpetergeschirr von einem Fleck zum andern. Da traf ich freylich allerhand Leuthe, immer neue Gesellschaft, und mir bisdahin unbekannte Gegenden an; und diese und jene waren mir bald widrig, bald angenehm.[52]

The biblical reference is low-key. The world is too interesting a place, too much is going on, for Bräker to give Cain more than a cursory mention. Bräker's mind is, as he says at one point, not on books but on the wide world. Hamann declares that the map of the Israelites' journeyings exactly matches the course of his life; his pilgrimage on earth will lead him to the Promised Land.[53] Here, by contrast, is Bräker commenting on the cheery hopes his dad and a neighbour cherished of the end of the world, as prophesied in The Revelation of St John and The Book of Daniel:

So viel weiß ich wohl, wir steckten damals beyde in schweren Schulden, und hofften vielleicht durch das End der Welt davon befreyt zu werden: Wenigstens hört' ich sie oft vom Neufunden Land, Carolina, Pensylvani und Virgini sprechen; ein andermal überhaupt von einer Flucht, vom Auszug aus Babel, von den Reisekosten u. dgl. ... mein Herz hüpfte mir im Leib bey dem Gedanken an dieß herrliche Canaan, wie ich mir's vorstellte.[54]

The intensity has gone out of the age-old biblical images. Humour keeps on breaking in. At Pirna, before the Battle of Lobositz, the padre addresses the Prussian troops. There stands the squaddie Bräker with his Swiss mates, constantly on the look-out for a quick get-away:

Bis hieher hat der Herr geholfen! Diese Worte waren der erste Text unsers Feldpredigers bey Pirna. O ja! dacht' ich: Das hat er, und wird ferner helfen — und zwar hoffentlich mir in mein Vaterland — denn was gehen mich eure Kriege an?[55]

Bräker is not taken in; he knows the way of the world too well. The Bible is, like anything else held sacred, something that people can and do use for their own sordid military or political ends. It is a book rather like any other book, a work of literature one can embroider upon or travesty to suit one's literary purposes. Nor was he by any means alone in this view. Listen to George Christoph Lichtenberg, writing not long after:

. . . die Bibel ist ein Buch, von Menschen geschrieben, wie alle Bücher. Von Menschen die etwas anderes waren als wir, weil sie in etwas andern Zeiten lebten; etwas simpler in manchen Stücken waren als wie wir, dafür aber auch sehr viel unwissender; daß sie also ein Buch sei worin manches Wahre und manches Falsche, manches Gute und manches Schlechte enthalten ist. Je mehr eine Erklärung die Bibel zu einem ganz gewöhnlichen Buche macht, desto besser ist sie . . .[56]

And so Bräker, writing of his relations with his nagging wife, whom he characteristically terms Dulcinea or Mrs Job ('meine Jöbin'),[57] using now *Don Quixote*, now the Bible as models, feels free to quip, after heaping insults upon her:

Doch im Ernst: — which one might render by the comedian's phrase 'But seriously folks!' — Ihre aufrichtig Bitte zu Gott geht gewiß dahin: 'Laß doch dereinst mich und meinen Mann einander im Himmel antreffen, um uns nie mehr trennen zu müssen.' Ich hingegen — ich will es nur gestehen — mag wohl eher in einer bösen Laune gebetet haben: 'Beßter Vater! In deinem Hause sind viele Wohnungen;' — an obvious reference to St John's Gospel chapter fourteen — 'also hast du gewiß auch mir ein stilles Winkelgen bestimmt. Auch meinem

Weibe ordne ein artiges — nur nicht zu nahe bey dem
meinigen.'[58]

We are now worlds away from the pious Hemme Hayen
and his wife. Similarly Bräker, in debt as usual, ironically
terms his constant response to adversity: 'God will
provide' — that trust in Providence found in so many a
Pietist's breast and, to a signal degree, in Jung-Stilling's
— a 'Waidspruch',[59] a rallying-cry, as if he half-sees
through his own psychological defences. In such sophis-
tication, such dissolving relativistic psychology, such
doubtless endearing, novelistic 'Selbstironie',[60] is not
Bräker pointing the way to Romanticism, that rich and
heady mixture, the moral and hence aesthetic disparate-
ness of the modern world?

How has this happened? One answer is that for the
articulation of his life Bräker has, like so many of his time
and after, gone to school to Shakespeare, rather than the
Bible. Goethe once remarked:

Wieviel Falsches Shakespeare und besonders Calderon über uns
gebracht, wie diese zwei großen Lichter des poetischen
Himmels für uns zu Irrlichtern geworden, mögen die Litera-
toren der Folgezeit historisch bemerken.[61]

In contrast to the stern absolute Bible, didactic throughout, with its repeated call for personal commitment:
'Go and do thou likewise', 'Be ye doers of the word, and
not hearers only, deceiving your own selves',[62] stands
Shakespeare, 'unser grosser Meister',[63] who, for all the
undoubted rightness of the total drift of his plays, sees
life primarily as drama, the world as a stage, men as
players, has a disarming habit of placing good advice in
the mouths of villains like the Duke of Cornwall, or
fools like Polonius, of letting outrageous farce follow on
the heels of blackest tragedy, of suddenly expressing the

most nihilistic of sentiments, of withholding any final explicit judgement. Liberating yes, but also bewildering — to view life aesthetically rather than morally. After all, one of the very greatest achievements of Judaeo-Christianity is just that — to view life morally.

Admittedly Bräker can and does at times write movingly of God's mercy to him, but he writes at a different remove from Bunyan or Hamann. He is a modern. A gulf has opened out between them and him, a difference in *tone* which springs from the difference in their attitudes to the Bible and God, and hence to themselves and their lives, for Christianity is, for good or ill, very much a religion of the book, a book to be taken very seriously indeed.

A new irony has come into the world, an ineluctable sense that there are more things in heaven and earth than are dreamt of in any philosophy or written down in any book. The Bible is seemingly losing its age-old sacred sway over men's lives. Bräker's irony, born of scepticism, differs radically from Hamann's irony which springs from humility. The suspicion is growing that the Scripture *may* be broken, that the realm of the ideal and the real do not and probably cannot coincide. 'Diskrepanz', 'Zerrissenheit', that 'dissociation of sensibility', of which T. S. Eliot speaks,[64] has taken place. Modern irony is its bitter-sweet fruit, irony and that eerie hypochondria that so often seems to dog it, as Mörike shows in his haunting modern autobiographical novel, *Maler Nolten*. — Hypochondria and artistic inspiration in place of the conviction of sin and grace. Seemingly only a novelistic treatment, not spiritual autobiography, could now do justice to the bewildering 'Raritätenkasten',[65] the 'Jahrmarkt',[66] the whirligig, the kaleidoscope, the labyrinth of human life, as seen, say, by Lichtenberg, the outsider, standing at his window. Phantasmagoria replacing allegory. Does not such an observation as Lichtenberg's: 'Dass in den Kirchen gepredigt wird macht deswegen die Blitzableiter auf ihnen nicht unnötig'[67] express in a nutshell this new knowingness, this irony that permeates even the very profoundest achievements of the late eighteenth century and later?

Elizabeth Avery, John Bunyan, Hemme Hayen, Johann Georg Hamann, Ulrich Bräker — I have come a long way, 'beginning in wisdom, dying in doubt'.[68] I hope, however, in the process a little light has been cast on Puritanism and Pietism — terms that have been used to cover a multitude of sins — and, more important, on the characters and lives of our ancestors sometimes glibly classified by these terms. Whether we like it or not, we are their heirs.

We live in an age in which the young clamour for relevance and contemporaneity, an indication of the confusions of our culture. What is more pressing a problem than man himself? — and here, Carl Gustav Jung warns us not to neglect the study of those who went before us along the path of life:

The less we understand of what our fathers and forefathers sought, the less we understand ourselves.[69]

REFERENCES

[1] *Experience of Elizabeth Avery* in John Rogers: *A Tabernacle of the Sun, or Irenicum Evangelicum: an Idea of Church Discipline, with an Account of Religious Experiences* (London, 1653), p. 403.

[2] 2 Samuel XII. 22, 23.

[3] John Bunyan: *Grace Abounding to the Chief of Sinners*, ed. by R. Sharrock (Oxford, 1962), p. 97 (referred to as Bunyan).

[4] Ulrich Bräker: *Der arme Mann im Tockenburg* (Munich, 1965), see Chapter LXIX, pp. 146–51 (referred to as Bräker).

[5] Hemme Hayen: *Lebens=Lauff auff Begehren einiger Freunden von ihm erzehlet*, etc., in Johann Heinrich Reitz: *Historie der Wiedergebohrnen* (Itzstein, 1717), V. Theil, pp. 169–99; here p. 171 (referred to as Hayen).

[6] Hayen, pp. 172 f.

[7] Compare Carl Gustav Jung: *Memories, Dreams, Reflections*, ed. by A. Jaffré, transl. by R. and C. Winston (London, 1963), p. 313 (referred to as Jung):
  Meaninglessness inhibits fullness of life and is therefore equivalent to illness. Meaning makes a great many things endurable — perhaps everything.

[8] Bunyan, p. 4.

[9] Hayen, p. 173.

[10] Hannah's prayer: 1 Samuel II. 1–10; Magnificat: St Luke I. 47–55.

[11] Bunyan, p. 98.

[12] Ibid.

[13] Ibid.

[14] Johann Georg Hamann: *Fünf Hirtenbriefe über das Schuldrama*, in *Hamann's Schriften* in 9 volumes, ed. by F. Roth (Berlin, 1821–43), Vol. II, pp. 436 f. (referred to as Hamann).

[15] Philolaoclerus: *The Private Christians Non Ultra or a Plea for the Lay-Man's Interpreting the Scriptures* (Oxford, 1656), p. 28.

[16] William Tyndale: *Doctrinal Treatises*, etc. (Parker Society), ed. by the Revd H. Walter (Cambridge, 1848), p. 463, quoted in Bunyan, intro. p. xxviii.

[17] Hebrews IV. 12.

[18] Bunyan, p. 43.

[19] Ibid.

[20] Ibid., p. 47.

[21] Ibid., p. 50. Here Bunyan is referring to Acts I.

[22] Ibid., p. 22.

[23] Hayen, p. 188.

[24] Maurus Berve: *Die Armenbibel. Herkunft, Gestalt, Typologie* (Beuron, 1969), pp. 34–45. See the picture facing p. 40.

[25] Hayen, p. 193.

[26] Johann Wolfgang von Goethe: *Goethes Werke* ('Hamburger Ausgabe'), ed. by E. Trunz, Vol. XII, p. 508 (referred to as Goethe).

[27] Hamann, I, p. 138.

[28] Hayen, p. 188.

[29] Bunyan, p. 65.

[30] St Augustine of Hippo: *Confessions*, transl. with an intro. by R. S. Pine-Coffin, Harmondsworth (1968), p. 216 (Book X, section 8).

[31] 1 Corinthians II. 14.

[32] Anna Trapnel: *The Cry of a Stone: or a Relation of Something spoken in Whitehall* etc. (London, 1654), p. 67.

[33] Bunyan, p. 3.

[34] John Collins: *The Weavers Pocket-Book or, Weaving Spiritualized* (Glasgow, 1766), p. 144. This is a later edition of John Collinges's *The Weaver's Pocket-Book: or, Weaving Spiritualized* (London, 1675).

[35] John Flavel: *Navigation Spiritualiz'd or, a New Compass for Seamen* (London, 1698), 'Epistle Dedicatory'. There was an earlier edition. John Collinges writes in his 'Epistle to the Reader' (p. 10 of the Glasgow edition) that it was Mr Flavel's *Navigation and Husbandry Spiritualized* that inspired him to treat weaving in a similar fashion.

[36] Bunyan, pp. 43; 44; 66; 76.

[37] Ibid., p. 42.

[38] *The New Science of Giambattista Vico*, transl. from the third edition (1744) by T. G. Bergin and M. H. Fisch (New York, 1948), p. 70 (Book I, propositions nos. 236, 237).

[39] *S. Francisci Assisiensis vita et miracula ... autore Fr. Thoma de Celano*, ed. by P. Eduardus Alenconensis (Rome, 1906), leg. I and II, p. 97, quoted in Erich Auerbach: *Gesammelte Aufsätze zur Romanischen Philologie* (Bern and Munich, 1967), p. 37.

⁴⁰ Hamann, IV, p. 278.

⁴¹ S. Aureli Augustini Hipponiensis Episcopi Epistulae, ed. by A. Goldbacher, Leipzig, in Corpus Scriptorum Ecclesiasticorum Latinorum, Vol. XXXIV, pars II, p. 191 f. (letter no. LV, xi, 21), quoted in Peter Brown: Augustine of Hippo (London, 1967), p. 263.

⁴² Hamann, I, pp. 445–51.

⁴³ Ibid., II, p. 198.

⁴⁴ Ibid., I, p. 212.

⁴⁵ Genesis IV. 11.

⁴⁶ Hamann, I, p. 213.

⁴⁷ Ibid.

⁴⁸ Psalm 16, 11.

⁴⁹ Bunyan, pp. 3 f.

⁵⁰ My underlining.

⁵¹ Bräker, p. 10.

⁵² Ibid., p. 175.

⁵³ Hamann, I, p. 216.

⁵⁴ Bräker, p. 43.

⁵⁵ Ibid., p. 110.

⁵⁶ Georg Christoph Lichtenberg: Schriften und Briefe, ed. by W. Promies (Munich, 1968), Vol. I, pp. 652 (Sudelbücher, Heft J, no. 17) (referred to as Lichtenberg).

⁵⁷ Bräker, p. 147.

⁵⁸ Ibid., p. 186.

⁵⁹ Bräker, p. 146:
   ... mich immer meines Waidspruchs getröstend: Es wird schon besser werden! Aber es ward immer schlimmer den ganzen Winter durch.

⁶⁰ Compare Willibald Schmidt's words in Theodor Fontane: Frau Jenny Treibel (Munich, 1966), p. 67:
   Aber das Schmidtsche setzt sich aus solchen Ingredienzen zusammen, dass die Vollendung, von der ich spreche, nie bedrücklich wird. Und warum nicht? Weil die Selbstironie, in der wir, glaube ich, gross sind, immer wieder ein Fragezeichen hinter der Vollendung macht.

⁶¹ Goethe, XII, p. 500.

⁶² St Luke X. 37; St James I. 22.

⁶³ Goethe, IX, p. 496.

⁶⁴ T. S. Eliot: The Metaphysical Poets, in Selected Essays (London, 1946), pp. 287 f.

⁶⁵ Goethe, XII, p. 226.

⁶⁶ Ibid., XII, p. 289.

⁶⁷ Lichtenberg, I, p. 860 (Sudelbücher, Heft L, no. 67).

⁶⁸ Robert Lowell: Tenth Muse in For the Union Dead (London, 1970), p. 46.

⁶⁹ Jung, p. 223.

Albert Verwey's portrayal of the growth of the Poetic Imagination

By Theodoor Weevers

THROUGHOUT his career as a poet, Albert Verwey took a profound interest in the nature and function of the poetic imagination and its growth. When, in 1925, at the age of 60 he was appointed Professor of Dutch Literature at Leyden, his inaugural lecture[1] was entirely devoted to this subject. He traced the origin of the concept of Imagination and its development by philosophers and poets. He showed that, for Spinoza, it was still an inferior faculty nearer to what Coleridge later termed *fancy*; that Vico in his *Scienza Nuova* (1725; 1744) first recognized it as an independent cognitive power; and that Jean Paul in his *Vorschule der Aesthetik* (1804) drew a clear distinction between the inferior faculty which he called *Einbildungskraft* and the fundamental power which he named *Phantasie*. This was the distinction which Coleridge adopted, using his now generally accepted terms *fancy* and *imagination*. We know that he shared and discussed his discovery with Wordsworth, for whom it became the central point of his poetic thought, and indeed the theme of his great poem *The Prelude*. — So far Verwey. I have reason to believe that in his view, Wordsworth there treated the very subject with which we are concerned. *The Prelude* is known to have been embarked on as a spiritual autobiography addressed to Coleridge. As he proceeded, Wordsworth became more and more concerned with what eventually was to be the sub-title of the poem as it was published posthumously: 'Growth of a Poet's Mind'. In other words, the subject of *The Prelude* was the development of *one* poet's mind, Wordsworth's. But he realized that much in this development was common to many poets, and indeed true of the growth of the human mind. In *The Recluse*, which, along with *The Prelude*, was to have been part of that much vaster poem which Wordsworth never completed, he wrote:

> Not Chaos, not
> The darkest pit of lowest Erebus,
> Nor aught of blinder vacancy, scooped out
> By help of dreams — can breed such fear and awe
> As fall upon us often when we look
> Into our Minds, into the Mind of Man —
> My haunt and the main region of my song.

Now Verwey, who was akin to Wordsworth and knew his work well, in the years immediately before 1920 — the year in which the poems were written with which we are concerned — had been making a close study of *The Prelude* with the intention of writing a full-scale book on it which owing to circumstances was never written; but, significantly, his notes and sketches centre round Wordsworth's thoughts on the nature of the imagination. He had also more than once written broadly autobiographical poems similar to *The Prelude* in manner and approach, though of far more modest dimensions. But, during a fortnight of July and August 1920, he wrote the cycle of twelve twelve-line poems that forms our subject: *De Legenden van de Ene Weg*. This is a work of an entirely different order. It is not a narrative poem at all. Each poem is separate, terse, wholly devoid of argument; each treats one scene or concept apparently disconnected from the others. One can indeed perceive connexions and even development, but these remain implicit.

Clearly, the form of Verwey's *Legenden* has nothing in common with that of *The Prelude*. Indeed I know of nothing comparable in Wordsworth, for in such cycles as *The River Duddon* the connexion is wholly explicit — quite apart from the fact that it consists of sonnets. But Verwey's cycle does call to mind the form of another poet with whom he had an affinity, Stefan George, his German friend, rival and antagonist. George's cycle *Der Teppich des Lebens* consists of twenty-four poems, each of four quatrains, whereas Verwey's *De Legenden van de Ene Weg* is a cycle of twelve poems of four tercets each. Formally, therefore, the two cycles are akin if not identical; but they differ in approach and content. Enigmatic as *Der Teppich des Lebens* will always remain, it can be seen to suggest a development which is cultural rather than psychological and spiritual. *Der Teppich* is the tapestry of life and art. It unrolls a veritable configuration of vividly portrayed people from succeeding periods of history: peasants, knights and ladies, monks, pilgrims, a-social wanderers, even criminals — then artists, poets, and finally seven symbolic statues embodying aspects of art. Each is a nameless, sharply outlined personality representing an aspect of past life or art. George's central concern is the development of life and art in succeeding periods *as these live in him*, and constitute aspects of his art. His art has the power both of evoking past life and of awakening yearning for it. He will make it spring to life, and even step out of the framework of the tapestry:

Da eines abends wird das werk lebendig.
Da regen schauernd sich die toten äste,
Die wesen eng von strich und kreis umspannet,
Und treten klar vor die geknüpften quäste,
Die lösung bringend über die ihr sannet!

This is part of the opening poem which evokes the overall tapestry of which each of the following pictures then forms part.

We shall see that Verwey's cycle is the realization of a widely different conception. He also, it is true, will be seen to suggest a development embodied in a succession of images. The nature of that development can be discussed better gradually, as we proceed to examine each poem. But one important difference is immediately apparent. The cycle straightaway takes us *in medias res* — it lacks an introductory poem suggesting an encompassing framework. Consequently, the images are not presented as flat pictures in a two-dimensional world. They are as it were suspended in space, and illumined by flashes of creative light. That suggestion of space is unmistakable in the first Legend:

HET STERRENBEELD

Het dal was donker en de weg was eng,
Hij wist dat uit de ruigten slangen loerden,
De hemel was een dunne en bleke streep.

Hij was gedaald: nu steeg hij, slank en streng,
Alsof de stenen hem naarboven voerden,
Een knods van wingerd hield zijn vaste greep.

En toen het scheen alsof op hoogste rand
Zich ogen brandend in de zijne boorden,
Hij toeslaan wilde op 't monster dat hem zocht,

Zag hij, zich neigend van de hemelwand
't Gesternte slingren, dat zijn gulden koorden,
Een labyrinth van licht, rondom hem vlocht.

THE CONSTELLATION

The way was narrow and the dale was dark,
He knew that in the thickets snakes were hiding,
The heavens were a thin and glimmering line.

He had gone down; he climbed now, slender, stark,
As though the boulders sped his upward striding,
His bludgeon, firmly gripped, a trunk of vine.

And when it seemed, up on the highest rim,
As though eyes burning bored into his eyes,
— He raised his weapon for the monster's charge —

He saw, inclining towards him from the skies,
The constellation winding, and its golden cords,
A labyrinth of light, enfolded him.

In its spare, austere form, two separate sestets, each
consisting of two tercets, whose lines rhyme in the order
a b c a b c: d e f d e f, the poem evokes an image of
primitive life. Primitive man, alone in his puny weakness,
bravely faces the unfathomed mysteries of the universe,
which he feels to be menacing. It is an image of primitive
life — indeed, an image of primitive *imaginative* life. This
man faces, not a cave-bear or mammoth such as we find
depicted in prehistoric drawings, but a constellation of
stars which his imagination views as a monster; and his
weapon is a trunk of vine — traditionally the poet's
emblem. He is a primitive poet, if only a subconscious
and potential one. As such he belongs to the distant past
— but also to the present, since individual man retraces

the development of the race not only before birth but also in childhood and adolescence. This imaginative savage, this adolescent poet, is gripped by numinous awe before the grandeur of stellar space. Being wholly inexperienced spiritually, he feels threatened by an unknown force, which his imagination visualizes as an immense monster with staring eyes. He prepares for a desperate fight against the luminous giant. But . . . the monstrous force proves benign: — it enfolds him in its splendour and mercifully spares him the hopeless struggle against supernatural might. — Man's individual will, though ready to resist, is encompassed in the Will of the Universe.

There is no doubt that both this poem and the three succeeding ones embody a stage of the human imagination which is not merely primitive but definitely animistic. The imaginary danger faced here is felt to be a monster. In the next three poems a rock, a mountain ridge, a tree are likewise pictured as creatures animated by living forces dwelling within them. Here is the second legend:

HET WITTE ZEIL

De rots schoof dicht. Als een spalier vol rozen
Rezen de bergen, hoog en eindloos ver,
Het land lag in een net van zonnevonken.

Hij die uit donker kwam bleef aarzlend pozen.
Van stroom en vogels schalde 't her en der.
Geluid en licht maakten hem stil en dronken.

Hij was geworden uit het ondergrondse
Tot de bewoner van dit tuin-heelal
En wist niet hoe; noch waar zijn schred te richten.

Toen zag hij waar de stroom de horizontse
Bergen doorsneed, ankrend voor havenwal,
Een klein schip dat zijn witte zeil deed lichten.

THE WHITE SAIL

The rock-face closed. Like espaliers of roses
Arose the mountains, high, immensely far;
The land lay in a net of sun-sparks sunken.

He, coming from deep darkness, wavering pauses, —
Roaring of rivers, bird-song everywhere,
The sound and light making him still and drunken.

From underground existence he'd arisen
To be a dweller in this garden-sphere
And knew not how; nor where to make his way.

Then where the stream cut through the far-away
Mountains, he saw along a harbour-pier
A small ship with its white sail brightly glisten.

Another image of primitive life. It always reminds
me of that wonderful statue by Rodin, *L'âge d'airain*, a
slender male figure lightly touching his forehead in
half-dazed wonder as undreamt possibilities dawn before
his mind. Like him, this wordless poet stands over-
whelmed by the beauty of the radiant landscape that
bursts upon him as he emerges from the ancestral cave.
But this time man is not single-mindedly fighting off the
mystery — he is reduced to wavering indecision, para-
lysed by rapture. Then his trance is broken by the sight
of the white sail: — a sign of the enterprise and the
co-operation of man with his fellows. Society, even if
primitive, now enters the field of the imagination.

The next poem is a scene of sheer horror. It evokes the terrors of barbarous society dominated by tribal superstition and magic rites:

DE BRUG

Zij grondden in de woeste stroom hun brug.
Maar dat er vrede en sterkte in 't steen zou wonen:
'Wiens liefste 't eerst hier komt, metsel haar in!'

De zon brandde 't gebergt op flank en rug
Toen zingend kwam wie haar gemaal zou lonen
Met voorraadvolle korf en kroes van tin.

Zij hieven haar — zijn armen hingen slap —,
Zij stelden haar in 't ruim, met voordacht open,
Zij metsten, metsten en haar blik werd groot.

Zij kreet — dit was niet meer een mannegrap! —
Hij zweeg en in haar hart verging het hopen:
Zij metsten, metsten tot de pijler sloot.

THE BRIDGE

They braved the raging stream to found their bridge.
But so that peace and strength should fill the stone:
'Whose love shall come here first, let's brick her in!'

The sun grew burning on hillside and ridge —
Singing she came who would reward her man
With rich-stored basket and a full canteen.

They lifted her — his arms were hanging limp, —
They placed her in the space, on purpose open,
They mortared, mortared, and aghast she gazed.

She screamed — this jest of men was growing grim! —
He stood dumb —, in her heart perished the hoping:
They mortared, mortared till the pillar closed.

This ghastly picture of the inhumanity of the age of barbarism is etched on the imagination by its starkly factual presentation. It goes back to a known source. Mr M. O'C. Walshe enabled me to follow up the suggestion made to me by Dr Mea Nijland-Verwey, the poet's daughter, that the subject was derived from a Yugoslav ballad. In this ballad (much too long and prolix to quote here)[2] a detailed description of the event is given, and — possibly in an attempt to soften the barbarous theme for a more humane age — the wretched woman is not immured completely but allowed a little window through which to receive food and to suckle her infant. The sacrifice is demanded by an evil spirit who keeps on destroying the foundations of the building. The husband, however, never questions the necessity of the sacrifice. With Verwey, everything is cut down to bare, wholly tribalistic essentials. He thereby situated the event far back into an age which mercilessly and with absolute conviction relied on human sacrifice to ensure solidity of structure.

There is no explicit comment. The stark factuality is never broken. Nevertheless the suggestion of evil is unmistakable. The poet's silence is a condemning silence — witness the contrast between the cacophonously voiced shout of the bricklayers:

'Wiens liefste 't eerst hier komt, metsel haar in!'

and the compassionate picture of the doomed wife:

Toen zingend kwam wie haar gemaal zou lonen
Met voorraadvolle korf en kroes van tin.

In other words, here is the poet's implied condemnation of an age that believed in the magic rite of immolating life in order to ensure the success of the urge to build. We in fact witness man's self-will setting itself against

Life in order to realize its selfish ends by *any* means, however inhuman.

It is in the fourth poem, *De Vogel*, that the oppressive earth-centred enclosedness of tribalism opens up to a sense of cosmic freedom. Two views of life are contrasted here.

DE VOGEL

In de oude boom fluisterde de Dryade.
Een vogel, blauw en goud, streek neer in 't loof:
Hij kwam door de ether, uit een ver vreemd land.

'Hij leeft door mij, ik gaf hem de genade
Dat hij nog groent. Hij kerkert me en is doof
Voor 't fluistren achter die onduldbre wand.'

De vogel zei: 'Ik kwam vandaag in 't reizen
De zon voorbij: hij zond zijn stralen uit
Van ster tot ster naar deze jeugdige aard,

En wáár hij scheen, ontloken paradijzen,
Gediert bewoog, kleur schoot in bloem en kruid:
Hij enkel wekte 't groen in dit geblaart.'

THE BIRD

In the old tree the Dryad's whisper sighs.
A bird, blue-gold, settled among the leaves:
It came through the ether, from a strange far land.

'It lives through me, the Dryad, through my grace
The tree stays green. It dungeons me and leaves
Unheard my whispers in this prison penned.'

And the bird said: 'This morning as I journeyed
I passed the sun, and he sent out his rays
From star to star down to this youthful earth,

And where he shone, paradise-gardens burgeoned,
The creatures moved, bright flowers and plants arose:
By him alone were these green leaves called forth.'

If *De Brug* was the confrontation of closed minds with dumb yearnings of love, in which the earth-centred urges won, we witness here the clash of earth-centred almost vegetative life with the growing imagination which for the first time opens up to the freedom of light and space. The Dryad embodies the short-sighted, self-centred mind which sees only its own efforts. She laments the tree's ungratefulness for what she regards as her own single-handed achievement. The bird, who has travelled through the sunlit spaces of the universe, knows that all life is engendered by the sun, that it is an unmerited gift to be received joyfully. The contrast is brought out by the antithetic first and second tercets:

(I)   In de oude boom fluisterde de Dryade.
      Een vogel, blauw en goud, streek neer in 't loof:
      Hij kwam door de ether, uit een ver vreemd land.

       (the lines suggest open space)

(II) The Dryad says:
      'Hij leeft door mij, ik gaf hem de genade
      Dat hij nog groent. Hij kerkert me en is doof
      Voor 't fluistren achter die onduldbre wand.'

and all her words are self-centred: 'door mij'; 'ik gaf hem'.

In the bird's utterance, we sense the liberation of the mind from earth-bound superstition.

We are now in a position to see that the *Legenden* consist of a succession of six *pairs* of poems, and that each pair is linked by a form of polarity. The single-minded pioneer who fights the constellation finds his opposite pole in another pioneer whose open mind drinks in the beauty of the world. The inhuman builders immure a loving, outgoing wife; the self-centred Dryad rebels against the imprisonment that is inherent in her natural mission.

Now comes a momentous step in this gradual liberation of the imagination. In the fifth poem, *De Gestorvenen*, man's mind conquers a new dimension. Henceforth he will no longer naïvely walk through an apparently endless stretch of timeless days. He now enters into the time-transcending communion with his ancestors, and — in the sixth legend — also with the loved ones who will survive him. This mental conquest brings with it a new form of thought: meditation.

DE GESTORVENEN

Wij voeden daaglijks met ons bloed de geesten
Van de gestorvenen, die in ons wonen:
Zij hebben aan ons doen en lijden deel.

Hun strijd is de onze en achter onze feesten
Is hun stille bestaan troosten of honen,
Hun adem klopt in 't lied uit onze keel.

Maar zij zijn blind. Wij hebben de ogen open
En 't heel heelal is in hun straal ons eigen,
Wij zien de wegen gaan van ster tot ster.

Deze zijn de onze en deze te belopen
Maakt de verrukkingen van 't droomzwaar zwijgen
Dat geesten doen, klaarder en lieflijker.

THE DEPARTED

We daily nurture with our blood the spirits
Of the departed, who in us live on:
They share in all we do and all we bear.

Their fight is ours and deep behind our cheer
Their still existence stands, solace or scorn —
As our voice sings, their breath within us stirs it.

But they are blind. Our eyes are open, keen,
And all the world within their gaze is ours,
We see the ways that lead from star to stars.

These ways are ours, and along these our course
Renders the rapturously dream-weighed hours
Of silent spirits sweeter and more serene.

Here the imagination of youth — both the youth of the individual and of mankind — truly grows up, and with maturity comes conscious poet-hood, the utterance in song: 'Hun adem klopt in 't lied uit onze keel.'

At this point the primitive beliefs concerning intercourse with the dead and the modern conception of communion with them are merged. In the *Odyssey*[3] Odysseus is unable to hold converse with the dead in Hades until the spirits have drunk the blood of slaughtered animals. Here the dead are felt to dwell within us, nurtured by our blood. That is a modern imaginative concept. The living blood in our bodies maintains the life of the departed who live on in our imagination, with that life of memory which Proust revealed in *A la recherche du temps perdu*. (I am not suggesting *influence* of Proust here, merely observing an affinity of thought which is not unique; Bisson has pointed to a similar experience in George Eliot in the first chapter of *The Mill on the Floss*.)

The growth of the imagination takes another big stride in the sixth legend, *De Gerichte Wil*. The poet's communion with past generations is established; he now discerns the link with posterity. And for the first time he speaks as an individual person:

DE GERICHTE WIL

Wanneer ik stierf en zij die mij beminden
Rondom mijn baar staan en de een d'andre vraagt:
Wat hadt ge lief in hem: zijn menslijkheid,

Zijn dichterlijke gaaf, zijn trouw aan vrinden,
De zachtheid van een kracht die draagt en schraagt,
Of de onafhanklijkheid van zijn beleid,—

Dan hoop ik dat een zeggen zal: wij weten
Dat hij als mens, dichter en vriend, als kracht
En leider 't zijne deed, maar nu de spil

Van 't denken stilstaat en in zelfvergeten
Zijn mond zich sloot, zien wij zijn sterkste macht:
Een op de onsterflijkheid gerichte wil.

THE FIXED WILL

When I have died and those who loved me stand
Around my bier —, when maybe one will ask:
'What did you love in him: his human-kindness,

His poet's gift, his faithfulness to friends,
The gentle strength that bears and shares distress,
The vision wherewith he fulfilled his task',—

Then one, I hope, 'we know indeed' will answer
'That as man, poet, friend, and as a guide,
A force, he did his part; but now that still

The wheel of thought stands and in self-surrender
His mouth has closed, we see his strongest might:
Upon Eternal Life he'd fixed his will.'

It is inherent in poetic maturity as it is in maturity
generally, that the mature poet is and feels distinct from

his fellows and must, literally and figuratively, speak for himself. The poet of primitive tribal society represents the corporate personality of the tribe; he says 'We'; the modern poet, however deeply he may share imaginatively in the joys and sorrows of others, knows himself to be separate and distinct from them; he must speak in his own person. This is why the latter poems of the cycle are different in character. One critic, Vestdijk, regarded this as a flaw. In his opinion there was a rift somewhere near the middle of the cycle. He went so far as to assert that at this point the poet had 'deviated from his intention of portraying the development of human thought in a series of mythological poems'.[4] This view to my mind had its origin in a double misconception. In the first place Verwey, as he indicated by his title, wrote *legends*, not necessarily on mythological subjects — in fact only one, *Orpheus*, is clearly based on a known myth. But moreover, he was, as we have seen, concerned not so much with the growth of thought as of the imagination. I would suggest that what appeared to Vestdijk to be a rift is in reality the inevitable transition from the approach of the primitive poet who voices the corporate personality of the tribe to the personal approach of the modern poet, who may and often does identify himself compassionately with others but nevertheless speaks as an individual man.

That all the imaginative persons who appear or speak — anonymously — in these poems are of the spiritual, religious type, is clear. The as yet wordless poet who in *Het Sterrenbeeld* faced the celestial monster was potentially religious: he was subconsciously aware of the Spirit of the Universe, and his resistance can be seen as a refusal to submit to an unacknowledged attraction. Verwey is a poet of this type; and it is as a poet who voices the human imagination in its religious aspect that he speaks in those poems couched in the first person. Here, facing his own death and pondering on the image of him that will be remembered by future generations, the poet hopes they will recognize that his entire creative will was focused on immortality, 'op de onsterflijkheid' — that is, *not* on poetic immortality, lasting fame, as it was understood by Petrarch and the Renaissance poets, but on the fact that in his work he embodied those timeless moments of ecstasy that are in fact moments of eternity.

It is now clear that my initial formula 'the growth of the poetic imagination', is rather too wide, since imagination in a general sense is not necessarily religious. In these poems it *is*, at first potentially, but then consciously so. They embody stages in the growth of that type of imagination, a growth which is a quest — at first a quest of something only dimly apprehended; but as the cycle unrolls it becomes a quest of the ultimate power that inspires the poet. In the first four poems the subconscious quest appears as a striving to conquer terrestial space; it is with that aim that the pioneer in *Het Sterrenbeeld* strides up the narrow valley, and that his counterpart in the next poem is attracted by the white sail in the distance. Even the inhuman bricklayers perform their nefarious rite in order to safeguard the bridge which is to carry the road that will extend their power on earth. But, unknown to all these pioneers, there was in that horizontal drive for power an upward striving towards the light — the light unwillingly faced by the defier of the celestial monster, the light that dazzled the pioneer emerging from his underground cave, and which was hailed by the bird as the origin of all life. At this point that urge becomes conscious. The poet Vondel, the protagonist in the seventh legend, *Rijpheid*, who lost his wife in middle age, is known to have felt the attraction of the poetess Maria Tesselschade, whom he sometimes addressed under the name 'Eusebia'.[5] Feeling himself to be on the verge of a passion that would have drawn him back to the outgrown stage of young manhood and thus destroyed the quest for the heights of poetry to which he was now dedicated, he resolutely turned away from this nascent love:

RIJPHEID

'Eusebia, laat los!' Die kreet van Vondel
Toen hij vooraanging in het vast besluit
Voortaan alleen te leven als gewijde

En lust en leed, te lang gedragen bondel,
Afwierp, opdat zijn geest, door niets gestuit,
De klaarheid won waar hij zich heel bevrijdde,

Die kreet klinkt weer wáár eedlen, rijp en ouder,
De wereld weten, en hun liefst geloof
Vervolgen willen op gedroomde bergen.

Zij voelen vleugels wassen aan hun schouder
En zijn voor 't schreien van de harten doof
Die hun de vreugd van 't dal nog eenmaal vergen.

MATURITY

'Eusebia, let go!' That cry from Vondel
As he forged onward with the firm decree
Henceforth to live alone and dedicated,

Having shed griefs' and pleasures' long-borne bundle,
So that his spirit, now entirely free,
Might win the clarity that liberated,

8

That cry is heard again where poets, older,
Mature, have known the world, and will pursue
Their chosen faith on visionary heights.

They feel how wings are growing from their shoulder,
Deaf to the weeping hearts that fain would sue
Them to enjoy once more the vale's delights.

Such a victory over self, such ruthless consistency is
rare. Immediately the pendulum swings back. The next
legend brings a sorrowful evocation of the mythical
poet undone by the great love which he strove to pursue
and recover even beyond death — Orpheus:

ORFEUS

Had Orfeus niet Eurydice gedood
Door zelf te hunkren naar haar levende ogen,
Voor eeuwig had hij haar in 't licht gevoerd.

Nu stond hij wenend waar zich de afgrond sloot
En had voorgoed zich aan zijn arm onttogen
Wie hij zo vast zich dacht aan 't hart gesnoerd.

Nu bleef zijn hunkren als een open wond
En 't lied van nederwaarts gericht verlangen
Zwaar en verzadigd, als een boom die treurt,

Terwijl die Andre opnieuw de cirkling bond
Waaruit alleen de opvaart van zijn gezangen
Haar — voor hoe kort, helaas! — had losgescheurd.

ORPHEUS

If Orpheus had not killed Eurydice
By wanting for himself her living eyes,
For ever he'd have raised her to the light.

Now he stood weeping where earth closed, and she
Had for all time withdrawn from his embrace
Whom he thought clasped unto his heart so tight.

Yearning alone remained, an open wound,
And his laments of downward-reaching longing,
Drooping and heavy, were like trees that mourn,

Whereas that Other One was once more bound
In the closed ring whence by his soaring singing
— Ah, for how brief a span! — she had been torn.

The thought is clear and profound: song perpetuates
but yearning kills. The musical ecstasy of Orpheus could
have perpetuated his beloved in a timeless eternity of
song; but his yearning for her living eyes drew her down,
away from his embrace — once more to be that other
Eurydice, the departed spirit, and to complete the millenial
cycle of which Virgil speaks in the sixth book of the
Aeneid: 'All these spirits, when they have rolled time's
wheel through a thousand years, are summoned in vast
throng to the river of Lethe, that, reft of memory, they
may revisit the vault above and conceive desire to return
again to the body.'[6]

By their vowel harmonies the verses underline the
dichotomy of soaring song and drooping yearning;
thus 'in 't licht gevoerd' calls up the contrasting rhyme:
'aan 't hart gesnoerd' — a vivid contrast between spiritual
exaltation and sensuous passion.

Poets, being human, may falter and fall — but the
imagination of mankind continues in its upward striving.
In the ninth poem, *De Stijgende Kracht*, the poet speaks as
the maker of a mountain lake in which his poetic power
is stored. The water of inspiration is not permitted to
flow freely towards the vale of earth; it is stored up in

order that, lower down, it may spring up as a tall fountain, the droplets of which sparkle in the sunlight, beckoning the poet's soul towards the expanse of the sky. But the water then rains down on the flowers in the dell, and the poet himself joins in the thanksgiving of the birds and flowers, since, along with them, he receives the celestial gift which came through him but not from him. He rejoices in being both a child and a lord of the earth.

DE STIJGENDE KRACHT

Mijn kracht, verzameld tot een effen meer,
Zal niet de tuinen in de laagte drenken
Maar enkel de hoogstijgende fontein.

Als ik mijn ogen naar de bergen keer
Is 't of de stralen mij als sterren wenken
En ik in hen 't uitspansel nader schijn.

Maar als hun droppling sprenkelt in het dal
En iedre bloem zich opheft in de gaarde
En vogels tjilpen in 't bevocht prieel,

Dan voel ik met een hart vol hemelval
Mij kind en heer van een gelukkige aarde
En luister naar haar dank waarin ik deel.

SOARING STRENGTH

My strength, gathered into a level lake,
Shall not assuage the gardens in the valley
But only feed the fountain soaring high.

When with my eyes the mountain-range I seek,
The jets of water, starlike, seem to draw me,
Until in them I seem nearer the sky.

But as their droplets sprinkle down on earth
And flowers lift up their faces in the dell
And birds are twittering in the moistened bower,

Then, my heart full of what from heaven fell,
I feel both child and lord of joyous Earth
And listen to her thanks in which I share.

But again the pendulum swings back. In *De Stijgende Kracht* the poet's imagination was able momentarily to see water, like heavenly manna, descending on earth. He now re-experiences the tragedy of Eden—the first heaven-drenched garden — where God would walk with Adam and welcome Eve, until the desire to be as wise as God destroyed the original state of being God's children and banished Eve and Adam to a realm of rock and thorns, of misery and death.

EVA

Toen God-zelf omging door het Paradijs
'Ik groet u, dochter!' klonk zijn groet tot Eve.
Hoe anders klonk daarna het slanggeluid!

'Gij zult gelijk aan God zijn, even wijs,
En niet een kind dat voor zijn Schepper beve,
Zo ge eet van deze vrucht, uw zoete buit.'

En ze at. En Adam at. En 't vurig zwaard
Dreef beiden naar een rijk van rots en doornen:
Hem die een god scheen, en haar, nog een kind.

Dat Moeder werd, die Kaïn heeft gebaard
En Abel, tot ellende en dood geboornen.
En Gods stem klonk niet langer in de wind.

EVE

When God himself would walk in Paradise
'I greet thee, daughter!' rang his hail to Eve.
How otherwise sounded the Serpent's strain!

'Thou shalt be like the Lord God, be as wise,
Not, trembling child, unto thy Maker cleave,
If of this fruit thou eatest, thy sweet gain.'

She ate. And Adam ate. The fiery sword
Drove both into a realm of rock and thorn:
Him who seemed godlike, and her, still a child.

Who grew to be a Mother and who bore
Abel and Cain, to death and sorrow born.
And God's voice rang no longer in the wild.

But once more, after this relapse — not merely a
mythical event in the distant past of mankind, but also
the experience of the loss of communion with God, an
event of which the human imagination cannot gauge the
significance until it has consciously experienced its
separateness from God — the upward urge resumes
sway still more strongly. It now becomes the mystical
urge to approach the eternal light. And this of necessity
implies isolation from other men: the distance between
the poet and the rest of humanity increases. This is
symbolized as an ascent into the heavens:

AFSTAND

Wie rijst ziet de aardse cirkel telkens wijder
En ruimer geördend land en zee daarin.
Hij kent zijn lieven elk op de eigen plaats.

Hij de Bevrijde wenkt hen als Bevrijder
En in hun hart ontwaakt een nieuwe zin
Voor de orde omhoog die zich omlaag weerkaats'.

Omlaag de volte, omhoog het eindloos open
Maar waarin elk die 't vindt elks ogen lokt.
En straal- en doelpunt wordt hij voor hun blik.

Dan daalt de ruimte en 't is als een ontknopen
Van strik en banden die ge rond u trokt.
En afstand wordt op 't woord: daar gij, hier ik.

DISTANCE

Who rises sees earth's circle ever wider,
More amply ordered lands' and seas' expanse.
He knows his loved ones where they dwell and go.

He, liberated, beckons them as Liberator,
And in their hearts there wakens a new sense
Of order, seen on high, pursued below.

Below's the crowd, on high boundless the space,
But who attains that height draws each one's gaze,
A lodestar, focal point for every eye.

Then space descends, as though you did unlace
The knots and ties wherewith you hemmed your ways.
Distance ensues the word: — there you, here I.

One man, the poet, is here seen to ascend ever higher into the boundless space of infinity — and inevitably, while his achievement is admired as a distant triumph, the separation, the isolation from mankind steadily increases.

The closing poem takes us into a yet more rarefied atmosphere, where all is shadowless light except for the distantly viewed turmoil on earth:

XII. DE HEERSER

Het leven is een schone en bloedige strijd
Waar alle om de oppermacht elkaar bevechten,
Maar grootste zegen is een vast bestuur.

Ik zie de woeling die zich wild verwijdt,
Maar in een Hand die wijs en sterk zal rechten
Hangt roerloos brandend de onafwendbare Uur.

De Heerser komt: zijn Vrede is niet de dood,
Maar de ongerechtigheid van 't tweevoud leven
Verslonden in een breukloos-rein bestaan.

Hij is die de Oorsprong ons weer opensloot.
De waan van Tweeheid heeft hij uitgedreven.
De Scheppings-daad heeft hij opnieuw gedaan.

THE RULER

Life is a beautiful and blood-stained war
Where each fights others for consummate power,
But greatest blessing is a steady rule.

I see wild turmoil spreading wide and far,
But in a wise Hand that shall judge and rule
Hangs moveless burning the predestined Hour.

The Ruler comes: his Peace does not bring death,
But drowns the unrighteousness of twofold life
In a new mode flawlessly pure and true.

He our First Origin re-openeth.
He ousts the phantom of twin natures' strife.
Creation's act by him is done anew.

The poem represents an essentially mystical vision which, being beyond sense, is necessarily unportrayable. One is aware of approaching it rather as the colour-blind must view the colours. But one thing is clear: far from being arrogant, the poet has here risen above his fallible self. Even so, he merely says: 'I see'; the mystical Ruler whose coming he announces is not himself, nor any individual person, but the Absolute Poet beheld in this moment of vision. What this Absolute spiritual Ruler brings is the healing of the breach in the human mind that leads to the opposition of the individual will to the Will of the Universe. He restores the integral wholeness of the Imagination which is a feature of the ideal poet, but which can only be realized in flashes by individual poets. That perfect integral Imagination would enable man to perceive all experiences of sense as intimations of eternity.

One is reminded here of Wordsworth's 'Intimations of Immortality'. But it should be stressed that Verwey arrived at this conception independently, along a development over several decades, which we cannot retrace here. Both poets' concepts are fundamentally religious; but, like Wordsworth, Verwey uses his own symbols, avoiding the current Christian concepts and formulae.

His images in this cycle adumbrate a development which in its essence cannot be portrayed because it is beyond the senses. It is symbolized here as a movement in space; from underground into the open; from below upwards; from darkness into light. Fundamentally it is what is termed in the sixth poem 'een op de onsterf-lijkheid gerichte wil'. This will towards immortality is remarkably similar to the urge which Friedrich Schelling in his *Philosophische Untersuchungen über das Wesen der menschlichen Freiheit* (1809) termed 'der Universalwille'. In his view this universal will is ceaselessly opposed by man's self-will (which Schelling calls 'der Particular-wille'). In man this strife is seen as the alternation of attempts on the part of man's individual will to identify itself with the Universal Will, and relapses in which the self-will of individual man opposes, asserts itself against the Universal Will which man is then determined to defy.[7] — So far Schelling. It is now clear that the fight of the lonely man against the monstrous constellation, the assertion of the bricklayers' tribe-centred determination to build their bridge even at the cost of human sacrifice, the Dryad's outcry against her ungrateful tree, Orpheus's earthbound yearning and Eve's eating of the apple are all instances of the rebellion of man's self-will against the Universal Will; in the case of the bricklayers and of Orpheus one might even, with Freud, define the event as the temporary triumph of the death-will over the life-will. It is equally clear that the cycle as a whole embodies the ultimate triumph of the Universal Will towards Life.

Whether the parallel with Schelling's thought which I have tentatively drawn is anything more than a parallel — whether Schelling's thought might have influenced the poet, is, and may well remain, an open question. There is no doubt, however, that for Verwey himself, *De Legenden van de Ene Weg* embodied a profound moral experience. In an essay which he called *Mijn Dichterlijk Levensbedrijf* — it was found among his papers and published posthumously[8] — he made the following comment on these poems:

When our whole personal life has got into a condition of disturbed equilibrium, when our destructive urge is carrying us away — what then is the only power which can restore our balance, resist our passion and stem it? We call it Will, and we know it only as the Will towards Deliverance. Of all the wills that work within us this one force towards redemption is the veritable will that compels us to find a notion stronger than all the notions that carry us along. This Will, viewed by me in a mode of thought not identical with those of others, is then the veritable Life, the God within us, understood not in his destructive but in his redeeming aspect. The writing of *De Legenden van de Ene Weg* was for me an important experience, because thereby, for the first time, I understood life as Will, and saw how I could portray it as such.

This comment by the author — which was *not* the starting-point of my study[9] — reveals a view with which the one here developed by me is, at any rate, compatible. It should be stated, however, that the poet did not intend his thoughts concerning this cycle to be read as an *interpretation* of the actual poems. In its context the passage is seen to be one particular instance of 'those thoughts of which the poet only became conscious through his poems'.

REFERENCES

[1] *Van Jacques Perk tot nu.* Reprinted in *Albert Verwey.—Keuze uit het proza van zijn hoogleraarstijd (1925-1935)*, ed. Dr Mea Nijland-Verwey. Zwolle 1956, pp. 12-33.

[2] See: *Volkslieder der Serben*, metrisch übersetzt und historisch eingeleitet von Talvj (Leipzig, 1853), p. 78, *Die Erbauung Skadars.* Dr Nijland-Verwey informed me that the poet's attention was drawn to this poem by a relative, the French ethnologist Arnold van Gennep.

[3] Book XI, ll. 96-8.

[4] *Albert Verwey on de Idee*, pp. 198-9.

[5] The poem unmistakably refers to Vondel's dedicatory preface to *Peter en Pauwels*, which contains the lines: 'Eusebia, laat los. Gij trekt my neder, / Die reede al uit den damp der weerelt was.' (W.B. edition, IV, 223.)

[6] Book VI, ll. 748-51.

[7] *Sämmtliche Werke*, Abth. I, Band VII, 5.

[8] De Nieuwe Taalgids, XLIV (1951), pp. 65-74.

[9] An earlier study of these poems, viewed from a different angle and with frequent reference to anterior views of others, appeared in De Nieuwe Taalgids LII (1969), pp. 81-97. This essay, which now places the cycle in a European context, represents my final interpretation and differs from the earlier one on essential points. My English translations are printed here for the first time.

Karl Wolfskehl. A Centenary Address*

By CLAUS VICTOR BOCK

KARL WOLFSKEHL was born in Darmstadt one hundred years ago on the seventeenth of September 1869. He lived to be seventy-eight; as Goethe said on a similar occasion, seventy-eight years — 'wieviel in wenigen Silben'. Wolfskehl might occasionally sign a poem with 'Aus der Wolfskehle gesungen' but the name Wolfskehl is not heraldic. It derives from the small market town of Wolfskehlen, near Darmstadt.

Family documents go back to the Germany of the seventeenth century. It is a family tree of distinction and it goes a long way towards explaining Karl Wolfskehl's proud affirmation of being German and Jewish at once. Even poems written in exile affirm: 'Ich bin Deutsch und ich bin Ich', or again: 'Wo ich bin ist deutscher Geist!'. He did not concede for one moment that a political party might decree who or what was to be deemed 'German'. If upstarts were going to lay down the law, he would claim, as a rejoinder, an almost mythical descent of the Wolfskehls from the Jewish family Kalonymos, who had settled in Mainz in the days of Charlemagne and Otto II. He was, then, an essentially proud man, with a strong sense of belonging, not easily uprooted, and with a sense of allegiance which did not permit him to change sides or to assimilate at will.

* University of London, Institute of Germanic Studies, 27 November 1969.

And yet the family of Wolfskehl had undergone an interesting mutation. When Karl Wolfskehl left Germany, his Dutch wife Hanna de Haan and their two daughters Judith and Renate stayed behind. They survived the war, and at the recent centenary celebrations in Darmstadt one was delighted to meet a whole clan of grandchildren, great-grandchildren and relatives gathered for the occasion. Several of their forbears had been bankers in Hesse and Hanover. The poet's father had been a man of public affairs, for many years Chairman of the Council of Hesse. His public service is acknowledged by Darmstadt's having an Otto-Wolfskehl-Strasse, named after him. But now, in 1969, one met an engineer, a schoolteacher, a student, several farmers. It may not be irrelevant to record that one Wolfskehl had to miss the reception given by the town council of Darmstadt because a cow was calving on the family farm in Kichlinsbergen, near Freiburg.

We know next to nothing about the poet's childhood, nor of the time he spent at the Ludwig-Georg-Gymnasium of his home town. We gather that he wrote his fair share of adolescent verse: 'Ich habe mir natürlich genug und übergenug in Knaben- und Pubertätsgedichten geleistet' — but not until he was twenty-three did he experience his moment of awakening. He refers to this as seminal and decisive: 'mein Keimerlebnis'. This was his encounter first with George's poetry and then, shortly afterwards, with George himself. The initiative had come from Wolfskehl. His attention having been drawn to the *Blätter für die Kunst* and to George's early verse, he sat down to write to the poet himself in Bingen. His letter is, strangely enough, a letter of apology, an apology for his own enthusiasm, his enthusiastic response to poetry: 'Ich habe zu meiner Entlastung nur anzuführen, dass ich mit glühendstem Eifer dem Sprung der Kunstentwicklung erkennend und geniessend folge, und dass gerade Lyrik das Gebiet ist, dem sich . . . meine Begeisterung zuwendet.'

A few more letters were exchanged. Then the two poets met in Munich in August 1893. George had just turned twenty-five, Wolfskehl was almost twenty-four years old. For the next forty years they were to remain close friends and collaborators. And in the fifteen years by which Wolfskehl survived George he constantly testified to the strength of the bond, calling himself an ever-faithful satellite — 'der Immertreue', 'der Flamme ganz Trabant'.

This unswerving loyalty, affirmed over and over again in letters and poems right to the end, was, I think, the value he esteemed highest, the foundation on which his sense of continuity and his self-respect stood firmly.

1893 was also the year in which Wolfskehl submitted his dissertation on *Germanische Werbungssagen*. It is centred on two medieval texts, *Wolfdietrich* and a narrative poem *Jarl Appolonius* printed in Hoffmann von Fallersleben's *Horae Belgicae*. For purposes of comparison and inter-pretation Wolfskehl drew on other tales of wooing from Germanic mythology and German folklore. Jacob Grimm's *Deutsche Mythologie* and Carl Müllenhoff's *Deutsche Altertumskunde* are two much-quoted sources and remained two of his favourite books. He knew them really well. And he obviously revelled in stories of dressing up and putting on masks, the countless Protean changes of the rejected lover who invents ever new forms of cunning disguise in which to win his lady's favour. The dissertation became, in fact, a study in hunters who were not to be caught and, by extension, a study in self-awareness. In his poem *Geheimes Deutschland* Stefan

George evoked Wolfskehl much later in precisely these terms, as 'der fänger unfangbar'.

I admit that I kept thinking of these words when trying to sort out what to say in this address and how to present Wolfskehl without oversimplifying him. I find myself readily caught by the spell of his personality, his outgoing, all-embracing nature, his sense of fun, balanced by his sense of dignity. On one occasion when a hostess presented him at the end of the afternoon with her visitors' book, he took it and entered in his almost illegible scrawl:

> Für 'ne Tasse Tee
> Verse machen — nee!
> > Karl Wolfskehl.

Late in life, the fun and effervescence naturally receded and the sense of dignity remained, heightened by the bitterness he had experienced. It did not sour him but it gave a sarcastic edge to his occasional verse. Here are some very late examples from his 'Bestiary' (*Biesterkunde*):

> Jeder Hund bepisst
> Den der Eckstein ist.
> —
> Jeder Faulbär brummt
> Wenn die Biene summt.
> —
> Aufgeblähter Gockel
> Meint, sein Mist sei Sockel.
> —
> Jede Mad im Käs
> Dünkt sich zeitgemäss.
> —
> Jeder Schneck beschleimt
> Was behütet keimt.

Which brings me back to 1893, the year of his 'Keimerlebnis', the year in which so much began to germinate and
to sprout. On the one hand, there is Wolfskehl's declared
enthusiasm for an as yet obscure periodical of contemporary poetry (*Blätter für die Kunst*), on the other
hand he is deeply absorbed in the study of Old Icelandic.
As a student of literature, he became neither a modernist
nor a medievalist, from which you may judge, with some
justification, that he never specialized. He had the
makings of a scholar but, instead, he became a lavishly
generous provider of ideas for others. He was, like
Herder, enormously receptive, and he had, again like
Herder, a quick, journalistic response. There are hundreds
of essays, articles, reviews, letters, which bear witness to
the astonishing range of his interests, his informed
hunches, his discoveries. He had his own ideas about the
weapons used in the Hildebrandslied, he argued for the
authenticity (still disputed) of an Old High German
lullaby. He sensed the importance of the Dutch writer
Van der Noot for the history of the German sonnet, and
he speaks of still earlier sonnets of the sixteenth century
(unfortunately Professor Scholte, the recipient of this
valuable information, forgot to ask Wolfskehl where
precisely he had found these early sonnets). His knowledge of Baroque literature made him a pioneer of
seventeenth-century studies; he probably knew more
than either Wackernagel or Gervinus, but unlike these
two scholars, he could not be troubled to write a history
of literature. His perceptive comments are scattered
through a sales catalogue, the value of which has been
recognized by its having recently been reprinted (without
authorization). Among the Silesians the sheer thrust and
fervour of Quirinus Kuhlmann's poetry attracted his
attention, and in the regions of Austria and Bavaria he

discovered an indigenous literature underneath the layers of Jesuit drama.

Together with George, Wolfskehl compiled an anthology of German poetry of the eighteenth and nineteenth centuries, which appeared in three volumes from 1900 to 1902. One volume is devoted entirely to Goethe, and is said to represent predominantly Wolfskehl's selection. And it was Wolfskehl who suggested the then provocative title 'The Age of Goethe' — *Das Jahrhundert Goethes* — for volume Three, which contains a severe choice of poems from Klopstock and Schiller — only ten poems by Schiller! — to Hebbel, Mörike, and Meyer. The preface to this volume directs attention away from Schiller as the popular author of 'Die Glocke' to his aesthetic writings and to the *Ästhetische Briefe* in particular — a shift of emphasis which has proved significant.

As for his own time, Wolfskehl showed a remarkably quick response to contemporary physics and its overcoming of the mind/matter conflict. He recognized and supported as yet unknown young artists like Kandinsky, Klee, and Franz Marc. These are merely examples, but they may serve to make my point: that Wolfskehl's is an essentially porous nature, characterized by a receptivity which he refined and developed to a degree at which it becomes creative.

His mode of perception is not easily defined. He is neither analytical nor descriptive. He seeks out points of convergence, likes to be generous in praise, and writes an evocative prose which combines fluency with the halting articulation of a stammer. His observations move rapidly from a far-sighted to a short-sighted focus, and back again. Facts become absorbed into myth, a sphere

9

in which he felt at home as a critic, as a poet and as an interpreter of his own biographical data.

To give some examples from the recent volume of essays and letters: An essay on Heinrich Mann opens with the consideration of 'Grundtriebe seines künstlerischen Schaffens', and ends with the comment: 'gibt zu denken, zu fühlen, zu erleben'. In another essay questions are raised like: 'gepackt? bewegt? einem geheimnisvollen Ziele zugerichtet?'. He feels something akin to the fluidity of Herder and Jean Paul — 'das Quellende', 'das unerschöpfliche ozeanische Fluten' — but he is not insensitive to the value of Lessing's more solid magnitude: 'gewachsener, bildgewordener Fels, ausdauernd und weithin sichtbar'. As for himself, he confesses at the age of sixty-three to being just as restive, just as curious as ever: 'zur reinen Privatexistenz bin ich noch nicht abgeklärt genug. Es zuckt, rüttelt, drängt und heischt'. After one of his meetings with Martin Buber he writes in 1929 that he feels less certain than ever of understanding Zionism, or of identifying with its aspirations:

Die Dinge gehen mir zu nahe, sie gleichgültig abzuschieben . . . Aber diesen Sinn, den tiefverborgenen, habe ich noch nicht vernommen. Und es soll nie vergessen werden, dass die sogenannte 'Zerstreuung' über die Welt, die Bindungen ans Menschliche, die Mitarbeit am jeweiligen Geistort kein Zufall sind, kein Übergang, keine Vorbereitung, sondern tausendjährigen Geheimnisses voll, Tatsachen eigner Idee, eignen Wertes . . .

Wolfskehl had already found his 'Geistort' and he did not believe in seeking another. In his essay *Begegnung mit Stefan George* he writes in retrospect:

Ich spreche nicht vom Dynamischen, der Stärke des Eindrucks, worüber sich ja garnichts aussagen lässt, sondern davon, dass

Georges geformtes Wort durch die ihm innewohnende Haltung Entscheidung heischend vor mich getreten ist, zu mir sprach. . . Plötzlich war die Welt zwar nicht 'vollkommen', aber sie hatte einen Sinn erhalten . . . Ich entsinne mich sehr genau aller Einzelheiten dieser Wandlung, die etwas vollkommen Neues aus mir gemacht hat.

The vocabulary used here is religious rather than literary. It is the language of the Acts, more particularly of Saul's conversion. What Wolfskehl seems to be saying is that he had journeyed and that he had come to his Damascus. The problem of how to be a Jew and a German was solved for him in terms of the challenge he felt when meeting George and 'die ihm innewohnende Haltung', in short, 'dass es für den Georgeschen Menschen diese Unterscheidungen nicht gäbe noch geben dürfe'. Martin Buber, on the other hand, had come to regard the post-Napoleonic assimilation of Jews in Germany as a grave error and a misdirected growth which had to be cut back.

Wolfskehl's 'Damascus-experience' agreed with Wolfskehl's essentially susceptible nature. He would not go in pursuit but would wait to be found. He did not seek things out, but would ask, fascinated: 'What is this now, coming my way?'. It was this susceptibility which George pointed to when Wolfskehl once wondered why George, who had, after all, the reputation of being difficult and uncomprising, tolerated and indeed esteemed him? George replied: 'Karl, weil auch Sie ein Ergriffener sind'.

Another related side of Wolfskehl's character was his immense generosity. George once compared his friend, who was so different from himself, to Diana of Ephesus, suckling all and sundry at her many breasts. Wolfskehl gave freely of his time and of his knowledge. He enjoyed company the way others might enjoy solitude. 'Menschen sind meine Landschaft', he once said.

The At Homes which he and his wife Hanna held in Munich have been described in several contemporary autobiographies. Wolfskehl, a powerfully-built man, over six foot tall, would meet his guests around the samovar set up in the drawing-room. He would stride up and down in discussion or listen with rapt attention with his weak eyes fixed intently on the speaker. He would find all the men 'unglaublich gescheit' and all the women 'namenlos schön'. The Dutch poet Albert Verwey wrote home after his first meeting with Wolfskehl in Munich: 'he seems to be always reeling, as if intoxicated, yet he remains entertaining and likeable, and when the rapid succession of his ideas comes out as impatient stutter, he appears all the more likeable.' And another visitor records: if you saw Wolfskehl with a glass of wine, you realized that here was someone devoted to wine. He hovered over the glass like a huge butterfly; 'schon wie er das Wort "Wein" aussprach, das verriet, wofür ihm der "Woi" bestimmt schien — zum seligen Genusse'.

The poetry of wine held a great attraction for him. He translated the Archpoet from Low Latin and the Middle High German *Weinschwelg*, and compiled a huge anthology in praise of wine from a number of languages. In the end, the vineyard became a symbol of his own existence. The grapes of Rhine-Hesse turned into the wild grapes of Isaiah's prophecy, but even these wild grapes he affirmed as a 'Spätlese' of some distinction. The opening of his Job-cycle, first published in 1945, reads:

> Tränen sind der Seele herber Wein,
> Fliessend aus des Leids uralter Trotte.

This looks like a metaphor — 'des Leids uralte Trotte' —

but in the next stanza it becomes clear that it is a per-
sonification. Suffering is the grape-gatherer himself —
'der Winzer' — and the owner of the oozing wine-press:

> Tränen sind der Seele herber Wein,
> Fliessend aus des Leids uralter Trotte
>
> . . .
>
> Winzer Leid, dich grüss ich, meiner Trauben
> Überschwere Beeren seien dein.
> Herbste! Lang schon gilben meine Lauben:
> Späte Lese bringt den vollsten Wein.

There is in Wolfskehl's late poetry a whole cluster of
images connected with wine. The references are partly
regional, partly religious, but when they become regional
as well as religious, a fervent topicality comes through:

> . . . Mich Keltrer, Kellerer des Weins,
> Des Weins, der Wort heisst, Geist, Tau des Gedeihns,
>
> . . .
>
> Mich wies ein Wicht in Acht und Aberacht,
> Griff mir ans Herz und trieb mich in die Nacht.

Treading the must, watching over the cask, serving as
vintner — 'Keltrer, Kellerer des Weins' — is one thing,
to be able to identify with wine is another. A late poem to
Christ, partly in dialogue-form, culminates in the con-
fession that the process of Wolfskehl's fermentation is
by no means over, the ferment has not settled yet, restlessness and agitation remain:

> Hast Du mich nie gemostet,
> Nie Deinem Wingert eingesetzt?
> Bin ich versengt, verfrostet,
> Dass Du mich nie gemostet?
> Nie werd ich Wein, ich weiss es jetzt!

Restlessness, an ever excited and excitable state of mind, assumed topical significance in the 'thirties. The cycle of poems called *Die Stimme spricht*, published in 1934, abounds in poems of exodus and departure; setting out becomes a form of life deemed sufficient unto itself:

> Fraget nicht, wohin?
> Wir ziehn.
> Wir ziehn, so ward uns aufgetragen
> Seit Ur-Urvätertagen.
> Abraham zog, Jakob zog,
> Alle zogen
> . . .

It would be wrong to deduce that Wolfskehl was a nomad or a vagabond. He may have been restless, but he was firmly rooted, and roots mattered to him. How, then, are we to interpret this theme of going forth? Did it come to the poet's attention as a topical theme of the 'thirties? and if so, did it clash with his imagery, or did it strengthen his regional and religious framework of reference?

The correlative between the imagery of wine and the theme of exodus may be found in a particular mood, in the emotional state of ecstasy, of being — if you permit a pun — 'transported'. It is clearly in the nature of our joy and our suffering alike to set us out of ourselves, beside ourselves. Again like Herder, Wolfskehl read the Old Testament stories as a record of spiritual experiences, of moods captured in archetypal imagery. When the Lord said to Abraham: 'get thee out of thy country, and from thy kindred, and from thy father's house', the corresponding mood would be: 'get thee out of thy self', and when the Lord said: 'get thee ... unto a land that I will show thee', this would signify: 'be prepared to receive my presence'. Looked at in this way, the change of locality, the wanderings of the patriarchs and, by extension, Wolfskehl's own emigration, become mental transports externalized.

Ecstasy is a state of mind which transcends our individuality, and in a way may be said to transcend the bounds of poetry as well. Nevertheless, Wolfskehl, like many of his contemporaries in the Expressionist movement, tried again and again to capture it. In a poem entitled 'Aufbruch, Aufbruch' he plays with the key-word 'aufbrechen' until it renders an unexpectedly fertile meaning: he must, as it were, 'get lost', lose his sense of identity, allow himself to be broken under the harrow like the clods of ploughed earth in springtime:

> Dass wir aufbrechen ... wie die Schollen
> Im Lenzsturm ...

The poem, written in 1933, fuses images of emigration with those of transport, culminating in an ecstatic sea-scape, with oceans of yearning and of frenzy, and a boat without a helmsman, tossed on crests of suffering, until dawn breaks and the storm subsides, and a more gentle rocking movement sets in. But this is where the poem itself ends.

> Fahren mit Ihm! hinaus! Allruf der Stimmen,
> Alldrängen unsrer Sehnsucht ...
> ... Was Steu'r? die Woge trägt. Wir schwimmen
> In Morgens Meer, wie schwillts von Fluten Harms.
> Meer, Meer wir selber, wogend in Morgens Schoss.

The title of this poem 'Aufbruch' would, properly translated, be 'Setting forth' (and this is how it appears in the English edition) but if one considers the rhythm, the swirl of imagery, and the ecstatic mood, one is tempted to offer as a meaningful mistranslation the alternative title of 'Break-up'. One may dislike such hazardous tendencies, or, alternatively, one can respect them, from a safe distance, as Stefan George did, when he told Wolfskehl early in the course of their long friendship: 'Dein leben ehrend muss ich es vermeiden'. The point I wish to make here, however, is this: that a lot of ballast was needed to keep such a mighty adventurer like Wolfskehl on an even keel. Over the years he had collected some thirty thousand books, pamphlets and broadsheets, most of them in the field of German literature; in addition, he collected such curiosities as walking-sticks, coins, snuff boxes, and a whole herd of his totem-beast, the elephant, in various sizes and materials. But when he left Germany for good on Shrove Tuesday 1933, the morning after the 'Reichstagsbrand', he boarded the train for Basle with a single suitcase. The next five years were spent partly in Switzerland and partly in Italy. In 1938 he consulted an atlas to find out how far away one could possibly get from Europe and embarked for New Zealand.

This brings me to Wolfskehl's last ten years, spent, as he once wrote, in the wedlock of solitude and sorrow — 'im Connubium von Einsamkeit und Weh'. His letters from New Zealand evoke in remarkably precise terms the changes he was undergoing: 'Ich habe mir selber Welt werden müssen, Geistraum, Wiege des Wortes', or, on another occasion: 'Man wirft jetzt soviel Ballast aus, dass man an der eignen Existe z sehr zu zweifeln beginnt'. One of the last photograp s shows him dictating to Margot Ruben at his desk. On the wall hangs a picture of Stefan George and an old map of the Middle East. Sometimes Herbert, a German gardener's boy, would bring him some plants. Wolfskehl liked and admired the rich vegetation of the Auckland gardens, and a Mediterranean fig-tree, growing outside his furnished rooms, meant much to him. He felt less at ease with the social conventions of Auckland life; they were unfamiliar and, one supposes, unexpected:

> Ich friere wo am weiten Ozean,
> Fremd mut ich, muten mich die Menschen an.

Moreover, his already weak eyesight was growing worse. He would now walk the streets with a white stick. For a time the New Zealand poet Rex Fairburn used to come for talks. Fairburn's volume of poetry, published in Christchurch, is dedicated to Wolfskehl. And during his last years Paul Hoffmann, then a student of German, used to cycle over every Thursday from a distant farm to see Wolfskehl in Auckland. Out of these regular visits evolved an as yet unpublished book on Wolfskehl.

From what his visitors read to him, Wolfskehl got a good picture of contemporary English literature. But without the motivation, the urge to translate was no longer there. Altogether, literature was no longer so close to his heart, and contemporary currents did not touch him as they had done before.

> Auf Erdballs letztem Inselriff
> Begreif ich was ich nie begriff.
> Ich sehe und ich überseh
> Des Lebens wechselvolle See.
> Ob mich auch Frohsinn lange mied,
> Einschläft das Weh, das Leid wird Lied.
> Bin ich noch Ich? Ich traue kaum
> Dem Spiegel, alles wird mir Traum.
> Traumlächeln lindert meinen Gram,
> Traumträne von der Wimper kam,
> Traumspeise wird mir aufgetischt,
> Traumwandernden Traum-grün erfrischt
> . . .

> Und wer mir Liebeszeichen gibt,
> Der fühle sich, wisse sich traumgeliebt!

This is an example of that rare second flowering called 'Alterslyrik', which was Wolfskehl's between the age of sixty-eight and seventy-eight. Like Job, he could say that the Lord had blessed the latter end of his life more than his beginning.

At the end of the War, when the question of his return to Europe was put to him, his replies show him torn between fear, pride, and a longing which never quite left him. In the end he decided against returning. He had, in any case, reached a point from which there was no easy way back:

Ein verstossener Dichter schleicht nicht zurück. Ich hatte die Zeichen zu deuten, ich hatte es als Wink zu verstehen, und als Ruf hatte ich ihm zu folgen, dem Ur-väterfatum.

Wolfskehl died in Auckland, New Zealand, in the early hours of 13 June 1948, at the age of seventy-eight. On his tombstone are inscribed his name, in Hebrew, and the Latin words *Exul Poeta*. They are neither German nor English, but these words say much — 'wieviel in wenigen Silben!'

BIBLIOGRAPHY

Karl Wolfskehl, *Zehn Jahre Exil. Briefe aus Neuseeland 1938–1948*, ed. by Margot Ruben (Veröffentlichungen der Deutschen Akademie für Sprache und Dichtung, Darmstadt, No. 13), (Verlag Lambert Schneider, Heidelberg–Darmstadt, 1959).

Karl Wolfskehl. Kalon Bekawod Namir. Aus Schmach wird Ehr (Castrum Peregrini Presse, Amsterdam, 1960).

Karl Wolfskehl, *Gesammelte Werke*, 2 vols, ed. by Margot Ruben and Claus Victor Bock (Claassen Verlag, Hamburg, 1960).

Karl Wolfskehl, *Briefe und Aufsätze, München 1925–1933*, ed. by Margot Ruben (Claassen Verlag, Hamburg, 1966).

Wolfskehl und Verwey. Die Dokumente ihrer Freundschaft 1897–1946, ed. by Mea Nijland-Verwey (Veröffentlichungen der Deutschen Akademie für Sprache und Dichtung, Darmstadt, No. 40) (Verlag Lambert Schneider, Heidelberg, 1968).

Karl Wolfskehl (1869–1969). Leben und Werk in Dokumenten. Katalog zur Darmstädter Zentenar-Ausstellung, ed. by Manfred Schlösser and Erich Zimmermann (Agora Verlag, Darmstadt, 1970).

Jan Aler, 'Symbol und Verkündigung im Lebenswerk von Karl Wolfskehl'. *Deutsche Akademie für Sprache und Dichtung Darmstadt, Jahrbuch 1969* (Verlag Lambert Schneider, Heidelberg–Darmstadt, 1970), pp. 164 ff.

Georg Kaiser Re-examined

By H. F. GARTEN

ON THE occasion of Georg Kaiser's 50th birthday in 1928, Brecht wrote the following:

Gefragt, ob ich die Dramatik Georg Kaisers für entscheidend wichtig, die Situation des europäischen Theaters für durch ihn verändert halte, habe ich mit ja zu antworten. Ohne die Kenntnis seiner Neuerungen ist die Bemühung um ein Drama fruchtlos ... vor allem muß seine durchaus kühne Grundthese, der Idealismus, unbedingt diskutiert und die Diskussion darüber zur Entscheidung geführt werden.[1]

Considering the author, this was an unusually generous statement. But it contains a subtle point of criticism which reveals an essential difference between the two writers.

It is customary to consider Kaiser as one of many playwrights of German Expressionism — perhaps the most gifted one. The peak of his career certainly coincided with the high tide of the movement. However, his beginnings preceded it by several years, and his work continued long after its end. The dispute over his place in the history of German drama has not ended today. Assessments of his stature are as divided as they were at the time of his first appearance. Some see in him no more than a clever technician, coldly juggling with ideas — a *Denkspieler*, as his first critic, Bernhard Diebold, labelled him; others as a visionary, impelled by a fervent passion.

Where is the truth? Closer investigation has been impaired by the inaccessibility of much of his work. Now that at last a collected edition has been published, it is possible to re-examine this work as a whole.[2] The first impression is bewildering. How can we find a key to this vast mass of plays, which comprise every conceivable type — social drama, romantic play, comedy, satire, history, and legend — yet all stamped with the unmistakable imprint of his personality?

Kaiser's personal biography offers no clue. He himself has summed it up in a brief abstract, which reads like the entry in an encyclopaedia:

Georg Kaiser — von sechs Brüdern der fünfte — wurde in Magdeburg am 25. November 1878 als Sohn des Kaufmanns Friedrich Kaiser geboren. Nach der Schulzeit im Kloster U. L. Frauen — das dürftige und ungeschickt vermittelte Wissen verdarb die Schullust — gingen drei kaufmännische Lehrjahre hin. Drei Jahre in Buenos Aires folgten. Klimatische Erkrankung brachte ihn über Spanien, Italien nach Deutschland zurück. Nochmals Jahre in Magdeburg. Fünfundzwanzigjährig das erste Werk — eine Tragikomödie von Krankheit und Verlangen: *Rektor Kleist*. 1908 Verheiratung und Übersiedlung ins dörfische Seeheim an der Bergstraße. Seit 1911 Haus für den Winter in Weimar.[3]

This summary, written in 1917, requires completion. Between 1918 and 1921 he lived in and near Munich; then he settled in a lakeside village near Berlin, where he stayed until his emigration in 1938. He spent the last seven years of his life in Switzerland and died in 1945, at the age of sixty-seven.

None of these biographical facts has left a noticeable trace in his work, which seems to be quite impersonal, the product of pure imagination. In a letter he calls all personal experience — school, friendship, love —

'Störungen' which the 'complete man' shakes off. 'Er kehrt immer zu sich selbst ein.' This withdrawal from the outside world into a purely subjective sphere is not only a significant factor in Kaiser's personal life, it is a keynote of his whole work. 'Der vollkommene Mensch' — this is a term recurring repeatedly in the few short essays Kaiser has written as comments to his works. These essays — a mixture of self-revealing flashes, pointed aphorisms, and flippant journalese — do not present a consistent theory. But they offer valuable insight into the working of Kaiser's mind as well as into Expressionist thought in general.

Kaiser stresses emphatically his belief in Expressionism as the only valid form of art: 'Expressionismus ist Kunst. Die Definition für Kunst: Ausdruck der Idee, die un-zeitlich-allgegenwärtig ist... Der Mensch (Künstler) weiß die Idee — er ringt um ihren Ausdruck. Erfolgreich nur im Expressionismus.' Expressionism is thus virtually identical with art. For art is 'die Ordnung des Wirrwarrs von Figur und Natur in die immanente Idee'. Reality is merely a 'Störung' which must be reduced to a minimum. But Expressionism is not only the supreme form of art, it is also unlimited in time: 'Expressionismus ist die Dauer der Kunst . . . Wir erleben die größte Epoche der Kunst: — der Expressionismus ist da.'[4]

When Kaiser speaks of Expressionism, he has above all Expressionist drama in mind — more precisely, his own drama. 'Das Drama', he writes, 'ist in dieser Gegenwart wieder Kunstwerk und Kunstwert geworden. Im Expressionismus . . . triumphiert Helle über Dumpfheit, Sprache über Gestammel, Ewigkeit über Epoche.'[5]

The advocacy of Expressionism as the supreme art-form has its reverse side in Kaiser's disparagement of Naturalism. He mocks at 'öde Abschilderei der Natur',

at 'Milieumalerei' and 'Zustandsanekdote'. His scorn
is directed not only at Naturalism as a literary style but
also at the favourite subjects of the conventional theatre,
in particular, erotic conflicts. He calls them 'Anlässe zu
erbärmlichen Spannungen' and goes on: 'Sie mit den
Mitteln der Kunst darstellen — heißt auf halbem Wege
stehen bleiben, Lyriker, Romantiker, Naturalist sein.
Halbwelt.'[6]

In contrast to realistic drama with its trivial conflicts,
Kaiser postulates the drama of ideas. 'Wer die Unzahl
ungedachter Ideen begriff, hat keine Zeit zur Liebe.'
Repeatedly he points to Plato's dialogues as the supreme
model of drama. 'Plato schreibt sein reines Ideenwerk
als Dialoge nieder. Personen treten auf und sagen.
Heftigere Dramen als *Symposion* und *Phaidon* sind schwer
zu finden.' The idea is thus the primary agent. It unfolds
dialectically, in thesis and antithesis, embodied in dramatic characters. 'Die letzte Formung der Darstellung von
Denken ist seine Überleitung in die Figur. Das Drama
entsteht.'[7]

It is this emphasis on 'thought' as the motive power
of drama which distinguishes Kaiser from most other
Expressionists. For one of the main features of Expressionism is surely unbridled emotion. However, Kaiser
disdains any distinction between 'Abstraktion' and
'Gefühl'. He speaks of 'die Sinnlichkeit des Gedankens'
and states categorically: 'Denken heißt: vital aufs äußerste
sich gebärden.' For him, thought and emotion are one,
or merely different degrees of vitality. In this sense, and
in this sense only, he calls his type of drama 'Denk-
Spiel', as opposed to the mere 'Schau-Spiel' which
satisfies the lower demands of the spectator.

When Kaiser was asked in one of those literary
questionnaires to name twelve immortal writers, he

replied: 'Ich kenne nur zwei Unsterbliche: Plato und Nietzsche.' While his citation of Plato refers mainly to the formal aspects of his drama, his indebtedness to Nietzsche reaches much deeper, to the very essence of his thought. His basic concept of 'die Erneuerung des Menschen', though closely related to Expressionism in general, has its primary source in Nietzsche. It is this concept which Kaiser claims to be the dominant idea — or 'vision', as he calls it — of all his works. Over and again, he articulates this idea in his essays. The diversity of his work, he writes in *Vision und Figur*, is a delusion. In fact, the 'Dichter' (he usually speaks in the third person) is impelled by a single 'Vision': 'Das einzig Eine zu wiederholen ist ihm bestimmt . . . Alles ist die Vision, weil sie *Eins* ist.' All his characters (or 'Figuren', as he calls them) are merely 'Träger der Vision', no matter from what period they are taken: 'Aus allen Zonen holt sie der Anruf — kein Zeitalter, das nicht einen wichtigen und würdigen Boten lieferte.' Thus, the multiformity of his plays is deceptive, for 'vielgestaltig gestaltet der Dichter eins: die Vision, die von Anfang ist'. In the concluding sentence he defines this vision: 'Es gibt nur eine: die von der Erneuerung des Menschen.'[8]

Kaiser is thus not so much concerned with the aesthetic aspects of drama as with its moral and ethical purpose. What matters is its activating effect on the spectators. Drama is 'eine Tat'; he speaks of 'Drama-Tat' and of the playwright as a 'Drama-Täter'. But what is the ultimate object of this 'deed' or 'act'? Kaiser defines it as 'Bedrohung des Zuständlichen', in other words, as a challenge to the present state of man and society. In this he clearly anticipates Brecht's theory of the 'Veränderung der Welt'. His drama, like Brecht's, is directed towards the future. But there is an essential difference. While

Brecht aims at the material change of society on Marxist lines, Kaiser's concern is the spiritual and moral transformation of the individual. This is what Brecht critically calls his 'idealism'.[9]

The question arises, what is the substance of this transformation, and what the image of the 'new man' Kaiser visualizes? As with every 'vision', this is difficult to define in rational terms. In an essay entitled *Der kommende Mensch oder Dichtung und Energie*, Kaiser provides some important hints. He uses the term 'Energie' to denote the vital power driving man on his road to perfection. For man is in constant motion towards an ideal future. The present, like every other epoch, is merely a transition to the next, higher stage of evolution: 'Der Mensch dieser Zeit muß sich entschließen, sich als Übergang für kommende Menschheit zu sehen.' The worst defect of our age is man's specialization, that is, his use of one faculty at the expense of all the others. This onesidedness vitiates his predestined wholeness. 'Der Mensch ist vollkommen von Anfang an. Mit der Geburt tritt er vollendet auf.' Onesidedness is imposed on him by economic necessity. The goal of man's evolution is to surmount this necessity and rediscover the wholeness which is his original destiny.[10]

This line of thought underlies several of Kaiser's plays, above all *Gas*, where the Milliardärsohn entreats the workers in almost identical terms: 'Sammelt euch aus der Zerstreuung — und aus der Verletzung heilt euch: — seid Menschen!!'[11] Or in *Gats*: 'Hört die Stunde, die mächtig läutet: der Mensch bricht an! . . . Ihr sollt den ewigen Menschen schaffen!'[12]

Kaiser's concept of the evolution of man is clearly influenced by Nietzsche — a name recurring repeatedly in his theoretical writings. But there is an important

10

difference: whereas Nietzsche's thought is focused on the
Übermensch, that is, on the superior individual, Kaiser
always speaks of *Mensch*. Of course, he too distinguishes
between the prophet, who is ahead of the others, and the
lethargic masses. But his ultimate goal is the 'wholeness'
of each and all: 'Fortschritte Einzelner werden von der
Gesamtheit eingeholt. Der Berg wird zur Ebene, auf
dem *alle* siedeln. Dann reguliert sich die Energie irdisch
und erhaben. Der Mensch ist da!'[13] It could be said that
Kaiser tries to fuse Nietzsche's concept of the superman
with the socialist ideal of progress for all. However, the
conflict between the individual forerunner and the
reluctant masses remains a central issue of many of his
plays.

If I have dwelt so long on Kaiser's theoretical
utterances it is because they offer important clues to his
work. This work, comprising more than seventy completed
plays, two novels, poems, and countless fragments and
scenarios, shows hardly any 'development' in the accepted
sense. It centres rather on three or four interrelated
themes, which recur with almost obsessive repetition.
Since he had the habit of reworking some plays, often
under different titles, even the chronology is difficult to
establish. He was over thirty when his first published play,
Die jüdische Witwe, appeared in 1911, and nearly forty
when he had his first great success with *Die Bürger von
Calais* in 1917. He thus did not belong to the young
expressionist generation — a fact which is of some
importance. By then, he had already written more than a
dozen plays, most of them anti-bourgeois satires in the
vein of Wedekind and Sternheim. However, these
contain one or two major themes which recur again in
the mature works. One is the antithesis of 'Leben' and
'Geist' — another concept deriving from Nietzsche.

Like Nietzsche, Kaiser extols the intrinsic value of 'Leben' as opposed to the deadening 'Geist'. This theme is struck already in one of the earliest plays, the tragicomedy *Rektor Kleist* (written in 1903), where the central figure, an ailing, intellectual school teacher, reflects: 'Was gilt der Geist vor der Tat? Lebe ich nicht — bin ich nicht das Leben? Und der Geist in mir das Tote, das mich vom Leben abzieht mit seinem Flug zum Tode — zur Ewigkeit?'[14]

The same antithesis underlies several of Kaiser's mature plays, such as *Die Flucht nach Venedig* (1923), which centres on the love affair between George Sand and Musset. Here 'Geist' is embodied by George Sand, who turns every experience into literature. She is 'der Tod in Weibsgestalt', 'der unmenschliche Mensch', from whom Musset flees in revulsion. At the end, she herself formulates her predicament in an epigram: 'Das Wort tötet das Leben.'

The supreme presentation of the theme is *Der gerettete Alkibiades*, written at the height of Kaiser's powers (1917–19). Here Socrates — quite on the lines of Nietzsche — stands for doubting, deadening reason, while Alcibiades embodies unreflective life. Socrates accepts death willingly to save Alcibiades, that is, the life and beauty of Greece.

Kaiser himself felt the conflict between 'Leben' and 'Geist' — that is, his work — to be one of his existential problems. Repeatedly he expressed his belief in the supremacy of life experience over his work: 'Keinem Erlebnis wird irgendein Werk gerecht.' Or, conversely: 'Das Werk — oder die Werke verkümmern das Erlebnis, das ich selbst bin.'[15] As he once put it in a pointed paradox: 'Ich möchte nicht mit dem Dramatiker Georg Kaiser verwechselt werden!' At other times, he tends to reverse the issue and consider his work as his only raison d'être. Whatever the order of precedence — the relationship between life and work, between 'Leben' and 'Geist', remains problematical for him to the end.

Another central theme foreshadowed already in the pre-expressionist plays is the breaking-away (*Aufbruch*) of a nondescript petty bourgeois from his narrow, humdrum life in search of a higher, fuller existence. In the comedies, the initial impulse is usually given by a large sum of money — the first prize in a lottery or an unexpected legacy — which enables a little man to rise to a higher social level. It is a theme that runs through the entire work, treated either comically or tragically. In the comic versions (*Der mutige Seefahrer, Kolportage, Zwei Krawatten, Das Los des Ossian Balvesen*) the man invariably renounces wealth in the end and returns to his former restricted life where alone he can find contentment. Thus, the comedies present as it were an inversion of the central idea of 'Erneuerung'. In the preface to one of his comedies, Kaiser himself puts it succinctly:

Der einzige Vorwurf von Dichtung: der ist die Erneuerung des Menschen — wird in der Umkehrung betont. Das Lustspiel verweist auf die Ernsthaftigkeit des Problems ... Die Tragödie bestimmt Aufstieg des Menschen in Bezirke des Vollkommeneren — das Lustspiel belächelt sein Verharren auf bequemer Ebene.[16]

The theme appears in its tragic variation in *Von morgens bis mitternachts*, Kaiser's first fully expressionist play. Here the initial impulse is not a lucky chance but a deliberate act: the Cashier, by absconding with a large sum of money, burns his boats; for him there can be no return. Trying to make up within a single day for a lifetime of frustration, he ends up disillusioned and shoots himself. In his final speech at the Salvation Army meeting, he draws the conclusion: 'Mit keinem Geld aus allen Bankkassen der Welt kann man sich irgendwas von Wert kaufen . . . Das Geld verschlechtert den Wert. Das Geld verhüllt das Echte.'[17] But what is 'das Echte'? The argument of the play reaches a negative conclusion. Material wealth and the pleasures it can buy cannot provide the true value of life. No positive answer is given.

The same argument underlies *Die Koralle*, but here it is carried one step further. The Milliardär, who has ruthlessly worked his way to the top of the social ladder, recognizes that all his wealth cannot truly satisfy him. He shoots his secretary (who is also his double) to obtain, by a mental *tour de force*, his memories of a happy childhood. For this crime he pays with his life. But he has gained a happiness he has never known before: 'Ich habe das Paradies, das hinter uns liegt, wieder erreicht . . . Ich bin durch seine Pforte . . . mit einem Gewaltstreich geschritten.'[18]

The notion of a crime as a means of gaining self-fulfilment recurs time and again. By deliberately violating the moral code, the individual seeking 'Erneuerung' places himself outside society. In the eyes of others, he becomes an outlaw, but he himself has reached a plane where the laws of society don't apply. The confrontation of these two kinds of morality, one objective and one subjective, is central to Kaiser's thought.

Both *Von morgens bis mitternachts* and *Die Koralle* may be considered as the first parts of two trilogies in which the initial idea is varied and developed. *Von morgens bis mitternachts* has its sequels in *Kanzlist Krehler* (1922) and *Nebeneinander* (1923). *Kanzlist Krehler* is of course little more than a weaker variant of *Von morgens bis mitternachts*, to which it is linked by direct reference. This time the central figure is thrown out of his routine life by the shattering experience of a workless weekday, which opens his eyes to the drudgery of his day-to-day life. He ends up in mental derangement and, finally, suicide. *Nebeneinander*, however, takes a new and different turn. Here an elderly pawnbroker comes across an undelivered letter from which he gathers that a young girl is about to commit suicide. He 'sets out' to save her life — the life of a complete stranger. His search is in vain. In the end, he returns to his pawnshop and turns on the gas-tap. But his ordeal, he feels, has not been in vain. He has gained 'den Gewinn des wunderbarsten Gefühls: für einen fremden Menschen sich auf den Weg gemacht zu haben!'

In this instance, the 'Erneuerung' implies the awakening of a sense of responsibility towards others. There is thus a distinct development from the self-centredness of the Cashier to the social conscience of the Pawnbroker. In a brief comment to *Nebeneinander*, Kaiser defines this development as follows: '*Nebeneinander* ist Endstück einer Trilogie . . . Langsame Vorbereitungen zu *Nebeneinander* sind *Von morgens bis mitternachts* und *Kanzlist Krehler* — *meine* Vorbereitungen zu mir selbst, der zum Pfandleiher des *Nebeneinander* vordrang . . . Ist das Resultat bedeutend genug, um ein Leben daran zu setzen? Ich überrede den Pfandleiher, ja zu sagen — und er haucht mein Ja in den Sonnenrest unterm vergiftenden Gashahn.'[19]

A similar development can be traced in the three plays usually known as the *Gas* trilogy: *Die Koralle*, and the two parts of *Gas*. These three plays are much more tightly knit, since they present successive generations of one family; but even they were probably not conceived as a whole from the outset. No doubt this trilogy — if we accept this designation — stands at the centre of

Kaiser's work. No other plays are more closely involved in the crucial issues of modern industrial society, and of man's position in it. The three plays encompass, in an abstract scheme, the evolution of this society from its beginnings to its foreseeable future: *Die Koralle* centres on the individual captain of industry who has worked his way to the top and tries to mitigate social inequality by charity; *Gas I* shows industrial society at the cross-roads; *Gas II* a future communist society under full state control. At the same time, the three plays mark a significant change in the concept of man's 'Erneuerung'. The Milliardär in *Die Koralle* seeks self-fulfilment by opting out of the industrial process and finding his salvation in a 'Paradies der Stille', symbolized by the coral he wears as an amulet. His son, the central figure of *Gas I*, becomes the apostle of a new social creed: roused by the explosion of 'gas' — the symbol of the machine age — he exhorts the workers to settle on the land in order to restore man to his pristine wholeness. His descendant, the Milliardärarbeiter in *Gas II*, accepts total mechanization as inescapable and calls for a transcendental ideal, culminating in the Christian message: 'Nicht von dieser Welt ist das Reich!!!!'

Thus, the idea of 'Erneuerung' undergoes a distinct development: in *Die Koralle*, it signifies the self-fulfilment of a single individual outside and against society; in the two *Gas* plays the imposition of his vision on society, in other words, the renewal of mankind at large. However, these two conceptions don't follow one another in successive stages; they run side by side through the whole of Kaiser's work. Significantly, the social aspect predominates at the time of the Revolution of 1918, that is, in the full flood of the Expressionist movement. The two *Gas* plays were written in 1917 and 1919 respectively;

Gas I had its first performance a fortnight after the Armistice and was immediately hailed as one of the outstanding revolutionary plays. Yet, in spite of his close involvement in topical events, Kaiser's approach is not timebound. The reality of the social scene — workers, factory, machines — is as it were metaphorical, a means of symbolizing his basic idea. Kaiser himself has formulated this in these words: 'Was ist Gas? Was sind hier Arbeiter? Mittel der Gegenwart, um ins Menschenunendliche vorzudringen; aus diesen Figuren abzuleiten das Gleichnis, das beständig gültig ist; den Aufruf zu uns, der so am schärfsten laut werden kann.'[20]

Clearly, Kaiser's conception is far removed from Marxist doctrine. His workers appear as a faceless mass, without a will of their own, rejecting the call for 'Erneuerung' and blindly following the devil's advocate who leads them back to enslavement. It is significant that the 'new man' never rises from the working class but from the upper classes — the Milliardär and his son, the Kapitän in *Gats*, Spazierer in *Hölle Weg Erde*, and so on. But also those who belong to the lower classes — the Cashier in *Von morgens bis mitternachts*, Kanzlist Krehler, the Pawnbroker in *Nebeneinander* — never stand for a social class but are always individuals in their own right, seeking their way outside and apart from any given social structure. In short, Kaiser's idea of 'Erneuerung' always applies to the isolated individual, even when he becomes the herald of a new social creed. The clash between this individual and society constitutes the main issue of most of his plays. Nothing could illustrate this better than the motto preceding *Gas I*, a quotation from *Die Koralle*: 'Aber die tiefste Wahrheit, die findet immer nur ein einzelner. Dann ist sie so ungeheuer, daß sie ohnmächtig zu jeder Wirkung wird!'

The call for social renewal falls almost invariably on deaf ears, and its prophet dies a martyr to his message. Only in one instance does he succeed in realizing his vision: in *Hölle Weg Erde*, written significantly in 1919, in the full flush of the revolution. Here a single man's appeal actually changes the hearts of men; from an individual case, the action broadens into a universal 'Aufbruch'. Each and all confess to their guilt, and, finally, the call of the prophet rings out over the sun-lit plain: 'Die Erde klingt!! Euer Blut braust — denn ihr seid die Erde!!' The three words of the title correspond to three stages of social and moral evolution: 'Hölle' stands for the present state of society; 'Weg' depicts its conversion — the awakening of a sense of moral responsibility, while 'Erde' denotes the ultimate goal, the realization of the ideal. However, this play remains an exception. Its optimistic ending was immediately cancelled out by the utter pessimism of the second part of *Gas*, which ends in the total self-annihilation of mankind.

As can be seen, the form the 'Erneuerung' takes varies from play to play. What matters is not the goal but the very act of transformation, the moving from one plane of existence to another, higher one. This central idea has its obvious parallel in Christian concepts. There, too, we have the idea of conversion, the abandonment of one way of life for a superior one, the via dolorosa through a blind and hostile world and, at the end, sacrificial death. In several plays, this analogy is underlined by the explicit use of Christian symbols. The Cashier in *Von morgens bis mitternachts* dies against the cross of the Salvation Army, his last breath sounds like 'Ecce — homo'. Here the analogy seems rather forced, since there is little in the Cashier's experience to compare with the Passion of Christ. The Christian symbolism is more to the point in

Die Bürger von Calais — the first play where the idea of 'Erneuerung' is clearly stated. Eustache de St Pierre, one of the seven burghers of Calais — Kaiser makes them seven for important reasons — sacrifices himself to save the city from destruction and to unite the remaining six. Over his dead body, his blind old father calls out ecstatically: 'Ich habe den neuen Menschen gesehen — in dieser Nacht ist er geboren!' At the end of the play, the rays of the sun reveal a relief over the cathedral porch, depicting the entombment and resurrection of Christ. Here the parallel is clearly drawn.

The dual origin of Kaiser's idea of 'Erneuerung' — on the one hand in Nietzsche, on the other in Christian concepts — accounts for the ambiguity of his image of 'New Man', which vacillates constantly between two poles — affirmation and abnegation of life. In the course of his work, abnegation grows steadily stronger. In his later plays, the Christian connotations become more and more pronounced. In *Mississippi* of 1930 — his last major success before the rise of Hitler — a community of American farmers who have founded a brotherhood on early Christian lines resist a plan to flood their land in order to save the city of New Orleans. They see in that city a new Babylon, doomed to be destroyed by the 'long arm of God'. When, in the end, the dykes are blown up and their land is flooded after all, their leader asks despairingly: 'Haben sie Gott in die Luft gesprengt?'

Christian connotations are most evident in *Das Floß der Medusa*, one of Kaiser's last plays, written in exile during the Second World War. Here thirteen children are drifting in a lifeboat from a torpedoed liner. The eldest of them, a boy of twelve, resists the plan to throw the weakest overboard. When he fails, and the rest are saved, he exposes himself to the bullets of an enemy plane. His body lies on the sinking boat 'wie gekreuzigt'. The analogy with Christ on the Cross is explicitly emphasized in the last line: 'Wieder einmal ist es vollbracht.'

This boy is the last of the long line of figures who awaken to a higher moral concept, and die for it. As can be seen, Kaiser's idea of 'Erneuerung' continues undiminished right to the end. He was the only one of the expressionist writers who sustained the ethical impulse of Expressionism long after the movement had expired. Some critics have tried to see in his post-expressionist plays a turn to *Neue Sachlichkeit*, or have coined for them a new term, 'Wesensrealismus'. In fact, he remained at heart an Expressionist, though with certain modifications. Firstly, he tended to use individual names instead of the nameless types of expressionist drama, and to derive his subject-matter from actual events, from history or legend, instead of inventing abstract patterns. Secondly, his language avoided the excesses of expressionist diction, though still retaining its unmistakable character. This applies even to the last three plays where for the first and only time he uses verse.

In examining Kaiser's dramatic work, I have so far bypassed an important group of plays — those centring on the love between two people. This type of play forms a substantial part of his work, stretching from *Das Frauenopfer* of 1916 to *Alain und Elise* of 1938. All these plays have certain features in common: they are almost invariably set in France, whether they are derived from history or anecdote, or freely invented. Structurally, they resemble the 'well-made' play, with its strict regard for the classical unities; but their thought-content is unmistakably Kaiser's. Thematically, they are closely related: they are, in fact, variations on a single theme — the passionate love of a couple which isolates them from

the outside world, and which they defend at all costs from
any intruder. This love is not psychologically differen-
tiated; it is absolute and all-embracing. Although it has
sexual overtones, sex is not an important constituent.
What matters is the spiritual experience which raises the
lovers to a new plane of existence. Usually it is the man
who experiences this transformation, and the woman
who, through her self-sacrifice, preserves the image he
has formed of her. The title of the first of these plays,
Das Frauenopfer, could be applied to almost any of
them.

In *Der Brand im Opernhaus* (1918) the debauched Parisian
nobleman, who has married a poor orphan, realizes the
emptiness of his former life: 'Alles an mir ist verwandelt.
Ich habe mich — mitten unter euch — meilenweit von
euch entfernt. Ich bin an dieser Insel gelandet, wohin mir
keiner folgen soll.'[21] The island image recurs in several
plays, symbolizing the isolation of the lovers from the
outside world. 'Hier ist ein Eiland, das blinkt — draußen
verbrennende Wüste.' (*Zweimal Oliver*). Or in *Oktobertag*:
'Liegen Inseln im Meer, wo keine Menschen sind?'
Whenever the outside world intrudes, threatening to
disturb the magic circle, it is ruthlessly repelled — even
at the price of a murder. The young lieutenant Marrien
in *Oktobertag* kills without a moment's hesitation the
butcherboy who claims to be — and is in fact — the
father of his child. Then, completely disregarding the
consequences of his deed, he embraces the girl he loves
with the concluding words: 'Wir können leben!' Similarly, the gardener in *Der Gärtner von Toulouse* kills the
woman who has revealed to him that his wife, whom he
believes to be an innocent country-girl, has in fact been a
prostitute. His illusion is more important than the factual
truth. The most extreme case is *Rosamunde Floris* (1940):

here the heroine commits three murders — the last of her own child — when she fears the secret of her love to be threatened. This she does with the conviction of her complete innocence and purity. The night before her execution, she addresses her distant lover in a long monologue: '. . . Ich werde rein sein, denn mich wäscht mein Blut rein. Es säubert, da es ausfließt, dies Gefäß, das ich bin — gefüllt mit Liebe — wie die Liebe alles ist — und das Vollkommene so selten, daß man es heilig hüten muß.'[22]

Here the prevalence of feeling over reality is carried to the extreme. In the clash between inward feeling and external fact, which lies at the centre of all these plays, there is obviously a close affinity to Romanticism, in particular to Kleist (the only dramatist, besides Büchner, to whom Kaiser paid unreserved homage). What George Steiner said of Kleist's characters applies equally to Kaiser's: 'They experience illuminations of consciousness which blind them to the realities of worldly circumstance. The entire drama consists in their stubborn adherence to the truth of vision. At the last their intense reveries prove stronger than material fact.'[23]

The conflict between the ruthless pursuit of self-centred passion on the one hand, and conventional social morality on the other, often culminates in a courtroom scene in which two moral concepts are confronted. While the judges summon one witness after another to clarify the facts, the lover safeguards his inward experience, either by stubbornly keeping silent, or by piling lie upon lie. 'Die Lüge', as a critic puts it, 'ist der Schutzwall, den sich das Herz errichtet, damit kein entweihender Blick in das Allerheiligste falle'.[24]

There is clearly a close connexion between the plays centring on the union of two lovers and those revolving round the transformation of a single individual, and through him, of society. In either case, there is a complete rupture with accepted social standards for the sake of spiritual regeneration. Both types of play run side by side almost from the beginning. However, looking at Kaiser's work as a whole, a distinct shift from the social to the private plane can be discerned. The expressionist fervour which had spent itself in vain against the hard facts of reality, was as it were introverted. The vision of 'Erneue-rung', unattainable in society at large, can find fulfilment only in the intimate sphere of an all-consuming love.

Between 1933 and 1938, when Kaiser lived in complete isolation, his plays banned from the German stage, he wrote no less than five plays of this type — all of them marked by an almost pathological introversion. It is not without significance that three of them open in a hot-house — a scenic symbol of the complete isolation of two lovers in a cold and hostile world.

It was during these years that Kaiser wrote his only two novels, *Es ist genug* and *Villa Aurea*. Of course, the narrative form, with its slow progression, was foreign to his mind, which conceived the world dialectically, in the clash between antithetic ideas. In fact, both novels are virtually dramatic-lyrical monologues — the second a single fictitious letter to a woman. Both turn on the obsessive passion of a man who, for the sake of his love, renounces his past, his name, his very identity, to enter into a new life. Thus, these two novels belong, thematic-ally, to the long line of plays in which the 'Erneuerung' is realized in a consuming passion.

It was only in the freedom of his Swiss exile that Kaiser returned to the wider issues of the present day. The rise of Hitler and the Second World War were bound to appear to him as the utter negation of his vision of 'new man'.

The plays of that final period are all directed towards a single aim — passionate indictment of National Socialism, militarism, and the inhumanity of war. They consist either of satirical comedies or of serious parables — *Der Soldat Tanaka*, *Das Floß der Medusa*, and *Die Spieldose*. In the first of these, a common Japanese soldier has his eyes opened to the evil of militarism which thrives at the expense of the poor. Brought before a court martial, he challenges the emperor to vindicate himself before the people, and is shot. As always, it is not a social class but a single individual who rises to a new morality. In a letter, Kaiser draws a parallel between his soldier Tanaka and Büchner's *Woyzeck*: 'Der Soldat Tanaka erhebt eine Fackel der Anklage — gegen die uniformierte Feigheit — gegen den Absturz in die Soldaterei. Dies ist der letzte Grad menschlicher Entwürdigung ... Es ist vollendeter Woyzeck — es ist mehr als Woyzeck.' In fact, Tanaka can be seen as a modern variant on Woyzeck — but a Woyzeck who stands up to his tormentors.

At the end of Kaiser's dramatic work stand the three verse plays published posthumously under the title *Griechische Dramen*. His approach to ancient Greece is far removed from classical tradition. In fact, the three plays — *Zweimal Amphitryon*, *Pygmalion*, and *Bellerophon* — re-echo, in poetic and mythological terms, the main themes of his entire work. In each of them, a deity — Zeus, Athene, and Apollo respectively — singles out a mortal to take him under his — or her — protection. For the first time in Kaiser's work, superhuman powers intervene in human conflicts. Essentially, these three plays, too, turn on the idea of 'new man', only that now the mortal stands under the protection of a godhead. It seems as though Kaiser, at the end of his life, had realized that man cannot renew himself by his own power but can only be redeemed by the grace of God.

These three plays may be regarded as a link between the dramatic work and the more than a hundred poems Kaiser wrote in a single outburst during the last few months of his life. After hiding behind the masks of his dramatic figures, he finally revealed himself fully. These poems, cast in a strict metre reminiscent of Rilke and Stefan George, are agonized outcries unequalled in their bitterness and mental torment. Perhaps they are too closely linked to his personality to be judged as lyric poems in their own right. But they offer insight into a mind which had seen its vision obscured by an unrepentant world. Significantly, many of them invoke the Passion and Crucifixion of Christ.

Where does Kaiser stand in the history of German drama? There can be little doubt that he was the most prolific and most versatile of the expressionist playwrights. He was the only one capable of casting the white-heat of Expressionism in a solid, almost classical mould. Two formal principles can be said to work in his dramas: the white-hot passion of Expressionism and the calculated abstraction of cubism or of modern architecture. These two principles inform his very language. There is a clear distinction between the exuberant, metaphorical diction of the central figure — the 'renewed' man — and the clipped, purely functional speech of the other characters. Kaiser himself defines this dichotomy as follows: 'Kühle Rede rollt leidenschaftlicher Bewegtheit entgegen — das Heißflüssige muß in Form starr werden! — und härter und kälter die Sprache je flutend-überflutender Empfindung bedrängt.'[25]

It is partly this highly stylized language which stands in the way of a revival of Kaiser's work on the stage of today. There seems to be a discrepancy between the apparent realism of his characters and their artificial, non-realistic speech. But his plays, despite their close involvement in the problems of his time, are not realistic. They are parables no less than Brecht's. His characters are not human beings of flesh and blood, but ciphers, exponents of ideas. This deprives them of psychological nuances, of lifelikeness, which alone makes a dramatic character credible. His plots are calculated to the last detail, often balancing on a razor's edge. Always, the 'idea' is the primary impulse, its demonstration in characters and actions secondary. 'Ein Drama schreiben ist: einen Gedanken zu Ende denken', runs one of Kaiser's much quoted dicta.

This insistence on the supremacy of thought over matter is central to Kaiser's work. His belief that man is not determined by social and economic circumstance but can at any time 'renew' himself by an act of free will is diametrically opposed to Marxism. It makes him rather an heir to German idealism. There are certain affinities to Hebbel and Schiller (though Kaiser himself only acknowledges his indebtedness to Kleist and Büchner). It is perhaps no accident that the first play which bears his unmistakable stamp, *Die jüdische Witwe* (1911), is stimulated by Hebbel's *Judith*, although it overreaches and satirizes its model. His affinity to Hebbel is also apparent in his approach to history. For Kaiser, history is no more than a jumble of meaningless events, to be set in order by the poet: 'Er schafft Linie in den Wirrwarr. Er konstruiert das Gesetz. Er entschuldigt den Menschen. Er leistet Dichtung.'[26] But unlike Hebbel, Kaiser knows of no universal law which governs history. He sees the past through the eyes of the present, adapting and altering historical fact in order to convey his message.

11

What connects him with Schiller, on the other hand, is his emphasis on the moral purpose of drama and his bold employment of theatrical effect to make his impact.

However, these relationships are hardly more than incidental. Kaiser stands in the first place as an exponent of a given period in the history of the German mind — a period of violent social and intellectual upheaval. Though deeply involved in the conflicts of that period, he has his eyes fixed on the timeless issues of man and his struggle for a better world. Kaiser himself is conscious of this dual aspect of his work. A short essay on the function of the dramatist ends in the words: 'Ins pausenlose Gleiten von Werden geschickt — eine Welle des Stroms kurz festhalten: ist alles, was menschlich erreichbar ist. Diese Feststellung einer Sekunde im All leistet der Dramatiker. Mehr nicht. Alles darin.'[27]

What will be the final verdict on the huge body of work Georg Kaiser has left? Evidently, this work is full of unresolved contradictions. While he proclaimed the moral renewal of society at large, he sought fulfilment in extreme individualism; while he decried the deadening mechanization of modern life, he was stamped by this age in every line he wrote; while he constructed his plays like mathematical problems, he was driven by a white-hot emotional urge; while he pointed to Plato's dialogue as the supreme model of his drama, he used every device of modern stagecraft to make his impact.

Was he the creator of a new image of man, as he claimed for himself, or just a skilful playwright? The question remains open.

REFERENCES

¹ Bertolt Brecht, *Gesammelte Werke* (Frankfurt a. M., 1967), Vol. xv, p. 155.
² Georg Kaiser, *Werke*, 6 vols, Propyläen Verlag (Berlin, 1970–). Subsequent references are to this edition.
³ *Werke*, Vol. iv, p. 546.
⁴ Ibid., pp. 571–2.
⁵ Ibid., p. 576.
⁶ Ibid., p. 587.
⁷ Ibid., p. 590.
⁸ Ibid., pp. 547 ff.
⁹ Brecht's attitude to Kaiser, whom he acknowledges as his teacher, is ambivalent: he praises him for having made the theatre 'zu einer geistigen Angelegenheit' and for having 'jene technischen Mittel ausgebildet, welche die ihm folgende Generation für ihre (anderen) Zwecke brauchen wird'. But while Kaiser still concentrates on the individual, Brecht's concern is man in his relation to society. —The manifold relations between the two authors are examined in detail by Ernst Schürer, *Georg Kaiser und Bertolt Brecht. Über Leben und Werk* (Athenäum Verlag, Frankfurt a. M., 1971).
¹⁰ iv, pp. 567 ff.
¹¹ ii, p. 47.
¹² ii, p. 440.
¹³ iv, p. 571.
¹⁴ v, p. 271.
¹⁵ iv, p. 559.
¹⁶ Ibid., p. 556.
¹⁷ i, p. 515.
¹⁸ Ibid., p. 710.
¹⁹ iv, p. 583.
²⁰ Ibid., p. 566.
²¹ i, p. 722.
²² iii, p. 428.
²³ George Steiner, *The Death of Tragedy* (London, 1961), pp. 222–3.
²⁴ Peter von Wiese, *Pygmalion*. In *Das deutsche Drama. Interpretationen*, ed. by Benno von Wiese (Düsseldorf, 1958), ii, p. 335.
²⁵ iv, p. 549.
²⁶ Ibid., p. 577.
²⁷ Ibid., p. 591.

'Bless Thee, Bottom! Bless Thee!
Thou Art Translated'
Typographical Parallelism, Word-Play and Literary
Allusion in Arno Schmidt's *Zettel's Traum*

By Siegbert Prawer

WITH its 1,330 large and closely-typed pages, *Zettel's Traum*[1] is as huge a novel as any published in Germany since the last war; yet its plot-line is exceedingly simple. 'Das Verfahren des echten Realisten', Arno Schmidt has said in a radio-essay significantly entitled 'Nichts ist mir zu klein',

ergibt sich ihm aus der Erkenntnis, daß 'In Wirklichkeit' viel weniger 'geschieht' als die katastrophenfreudigen Dramatiker uns weismachen wollen. Das Leben besteht, was 'Handlung' anbelangt, aus den bekannten kleinen Einförmigkeiten: also verweigert man sich als Realist 'um der Wahrheit willen' der Fiktion pausenlos=aufgeregter Ereignisse (wobei die radikalste Kühnheit in Denkweise, Sprache, Architektonik, sehr wohl mit solcher, nur dem oberflächlichen Beurteiler befremdlichen, Handlungsleere gepaart sein kann).

This insight is applied to the novel in another radio-essay, in which Arno Schmidt has one of his literary heroes, James Fenimore Cooper, distinguish his own art from that of Sir Walter Scott:

Sir, hätte ich sagen müssen, es gibt zwei Arten von Schriftstellern: die einen ergreifen den Leser durch die mächtige,

156

wohlzusammenhängende, bedeutende Handlung. Bei den anderen aber ergibt sich die 'Fabel' aus den Zuständen und Denkweisen! Etwa beim 'Robinson Crusoe'; da geschieht auch nichts! Nur Züge der äußersten Einsamkeit werden versammelt; und eben der eine Mensch darin — und doch ergreift uns das Bild des einsamen Mannes im Sand aufs tiefste, und prägt sich auf ewig ein! Und genau so ist es in meinen 'Pioneers', die Scott damals beanstandete: die Denkweise des neuen Settlements im Urwald; und die Denkweise jener Zeit: ich brauche gar keine Handlung. Die 'Wahrheit' kennt doch gar keine Handlung, wie?![2]

The action of *Zettel's Traum* is therefore confined to the events of a single summer's day, from daybreak to bedtime, with a brief epilogue set on the following morning. The central observer, narrator and consciousness is one Daniel Pagenstecher, usually called 'Dän' — a writer of some consequence who lives a scholar-hermit's existence on the outskirts of the village of Ödingen. Dän receives a visit from another writer called Paul Jacobi, an old school-friend who now lives in the near-by city of Lünen, and who is accompanied on this occasion by his wife Wilma (another old school-friend of Dän's) and by their teenage daughter, Franziska. Paul is engaged on a translation of Edgar Allan Poe's works into German, and throughout the day the four of them discuss Poe's stories, poems and essays and what they may reveal of Poe's life and mind. They walk through a field belonging to Dän and elaborately guarded against campers, they visit the village, make purchases in shops, drink at an inn, visit a church, attend a fair, watch Dän's cesspool being cleaned out, have various meals in the open and in Dän's house. The adolescent Franziska is unhappy at home and thinks herself in love with the (very much older) Dän; Dän helps to make things easier for her at home by good advice and a substantial gift of money to her parents, but decides it would be wrong to marry or live with Franziska, even though her parents seem to have little objection. The two most dramatic events of the day are a mild heart-attack which reminds Dän that his end cannot be far off, and a misunderstanding which has Dän trapped in a ladies' lavatory and nearly arrested as a voyeur; and, in a final scene, Dän sadly watches Franziska drive away out of his life. Besides this, a foul-minded school-friend of Franziska's turns up incognito and tests Dän by pretending to wish to seduce him — an attempt at seduction he does not find it difficult to resist; there are various encounters with village and fair-ground grotesques; and the central characters are made to witness, throughout the day, ludicrously multiplied scenes of sexual or excretory behaviour such as are normally screened from all eyes but those of the participants.

Let us plunge straight in with a glance at the opening 'sentence' of the book. Immediately, an arresting typographical picture confronts us. Two parallel rows of typed lower-case 'x's' part in the middle by having the upper row moved a space up, the lower row moved a space down, for the length of sixteen letters. Into the central enlargement thus created the exclamation '- : king!' has been typed, enclosed in double quotation marks and followed by a dash. The left-hand margin has the words ': Anna Muh-Muh!', enclosed in single quotation marks, while the right-hand margin raises two queries: '(?:NOAH POKE? oder fu= ?))'. The picture made by the whole line can be taken in by the eye at a single glance, though the separate entries in central column and margins must be read consecutively. In the same way the eye can appreciate, at a single glance, that the manifold typed material on the opening page is held, as it it were, between the picture made by the rows of 'x's' at the top and that made at the bottom of the page by a rough sketch-map of the terrain the four main characters will traverse in Book I.

It soon appears — the first clue, in fact, is given seven lines below this opening one — that the typed row of 'x's' parted in the middle represent a barbed wire fence through which one of the characters, Paul, is climbing; the exclamation '- king', a truncated expletive, is constantly to be found in his mouth.[3] What we have here, then, is what the central character, Dän, the 'I' narrator whose consciousness provides our constant and unchanging focus, sees and hears during the early morning walk he takes over his field in the company of his visiting friends. While he looks at Paul climbing through the barbed wire, which is being held open for him in the middle, he hears another sound on which his attention is not consciously focused: the lowing of cows suggested by what we read in the left-hand margin, ': Anna Muh-Muh'. Immediately afterwards, the same sounds appear in the same margin in a different, English spelling — ': Ana moo-moo!'; alerted by the sub-title of this opening book,[4] we recognize this as one of the phrases invented by Edgar Allan Poe for the imaginary language of his savages in *The Narrative of Arthur Gordon Pym*, as part, in fact, of Poe's language of Tsalal. Dän's thoughts are full of Poe, and he transforms the very sounds of the countryside into an amalgam of Poe reminiscence, reminiscence of a not unusual woman's name, and the traditional way of representing the sounds emitted by a cow. While all this is going on, the right-hand margin shows Dän's mind musing on the exclamation '-: king'. Is it to be preceded, perhaps, by a syllable beginning with the letters 'fu', or has it something to do with 'poking' — a thought which again brings in a literary reminiscence, this time of the quaintly and suggestively named Captain Noah Poke in James Fenimore Cooper's novel *Monikins*.[5]

What we have, then, in this opening line is the evocation, through words and 'typograms', of a complex of sensations and thoughts that go on simultaneously in the mind of a polyglot man obsessed with literature, a man whose inclination towards verbal play is not checked by concern over the taboos with which society has proscribed certain words.

The mimetic-pictorial element of the opening page is matched by other 'typograms' (if I may so term them) throughout the book. As a motor-bike drives through a puddle, a spray of lower-case 'f's appears on the page:

$$\text{'f}_{f_{f_F f}}\,{}_f f^{fff} f \text{ durch die Füttse:!' (p. 690). The words}$$

'Stirne, Auge, Auge, Nase (spelt vertically instead of horizontally), Mund, Kinn' arrange themselves into the pictorial semblance of a face on page 712. 'Mükken', printed vertically instead of horizontally, repeated four times and arranged in three unequal columns, makes a swarm of midges rise before our eyes (p. 963). The Cleveland National Guard, as seen on the television screen, appears as a series of dehumanized faces each made up of two lower-case 'o's on either side of an exclamation mark (p. 1164). A frog leaps and the line describing it leaps up with it; a hand is cupped over the frog to trap him gently, and the line arcs itself upwards and downwards again to depict the cupping; the frog is carried up some stairs, an arrangement of vertical and horizontal lines appears to mark the stairs, with a series of ascending dots miming someone walking up them

(p. 1193). These and other mimetic typograms, used sparingly but with an enlivening effect throughout the book, are supplemented by advertising material, photographs, extracts from book-catalogues and so on, reproduced in the margin by photocopying and offset processes. This is one of the ways in which Arno Schmidt breaks up the uniform oblong of type surrounded by white margin that we have all become accustomed to expect in our books, and in which he acknowledges, therefore, the partial abandonment of 'linear-consecutive' habits of thought which Marshall McLuhan has taught us to regard as characteristic of our modern world — a world Schmidt cannot love (he has been as consistent as his hero Dän in railing at the quality of modern life) but whose pressures he acknowledges and responds to.

The image of *Zettel's Traum* we have gained from its first page — a central column of type containing the main narrative, with marginal glosses on both sides and pictorial elements supplementing those of verbal narration — this image is still seriously incomplete; for what is not illustrated on that first page is the way in which the central block of print itself divides at intervals in various ways for various expressive purposes. It is this series of effects to which I would now like, briefly, to turn.

One frequent use of such division of the central block into two parallel columns is once again pictorial: it depicts two characters moving away from each other, or performing different actions simultaneously (p. 64, pp. 431–3 et passim). On page 1166 the situation is more complex than that: the main characters are watching television and the central block divides into three columns. The left-hand column gives what appears on the TV screen: the erection of a prefabricated housing-estate somewhere in the DDR.

TÜR & ZWEI FENSTER
TÜR & ZWEI FENSTER
TÜR & ZWEI FENSTER
TÜR & ZWEI FENSTER
TÜR & ZWEI FENSTER

To the right of the column thus made up we are told what one of the television-watchers says to the other while they are both watching: '(: Erinners De Dich an die Häuser=vorhin?; in Scortlebm, Paul?"—).' That then is the middle of the central block of print. The column to the right of that gives us Dän's reflections, triggered off by the TV image he is watching: 'I wonder', he says to himself, with a satiric glance at methods of authorship suggested at the Bitterfeld writers' conferences, 'I wonder if the authors' collective [*das 'AuThoren=Cullectief'*] is lurking in the background, writing down exactly what the first or the second labourer is saying, or what the workers' collective as a whole is saying. And while these three separate but simultaneous things go on in the central block of print, the two margins are not idle either. The left-hand margin brings a quotation from Poe, about whom the central characters' thoughts revolve constantly on their day together. This quotation, from 'The Devil in the Belfry', is once again clearly suggested by the image that appears on the TV screen. 'Every house has a small garden before it, with a circular path, a sun-dial, and 24 cabbages. The buildings themselves are so precisely alike that one can in no manner be distinguished from the other'; and since Dän's thoughts are always running on the psychology of authorship, he goes on to speculate — and this too appears in the left-hand margin — that Poe's description may have been influenced by the sight or recollection of a circular time-piece: 'Ein hübsches Beispiel der Vergrößerung eines

Uhrenzifferblattes bis zu den Ausmaßen einer lütten Landschaft.'[6] That was the left-hand margin; the right-hand margin brings yet another literary reminiscence triggered off by the sight of the prefabricated housing-estate, but this time, though there is a political point in the choice of a passage that speaks of 'multitudes . . . working incessant' and of 'slaves . . . oppressed', the connexion is one of contrast rather than likeness. It comes from Blake's *Vala*:

> Then rose the Builders. First the Architect divine his plan unfolds. The wond'rous scaffold reared all round the infinite, quadrangular the building rose, the heavens squared by a line, Trigones and Cubes divide the elements in finite bonds. Multitudes without number work incessant: the hewn stone is placed in beds of mortar . . . : severe the labour! Female slaves the mortar trod oppressed. — Twelve halls after the names of his twelve sons composed the wondrous building; and three central domes after the names of his three daughters . . . Every hall surrounded by bright Paradises of Delight . . .

We have then, in the passage just quoted, an even more complex but not radically different effect from that of the three-tiered arrangement we examined on the opening page: not three but five columns of typed matter are arranged side by side to suggest sensations, actions and thought-processes that go on at one and the same time.

One thing, however, differentiates the passage just analysed from the opening line of the book: its use of ironic counterpoint. The prefabricated housing-estate appears the more dull (if not any the less socially useful and necessary) when seen against the background of Blake's bright Paradises of Delight; while on the other hand, the housing-estate reality relativizes Blake's fantasy and that of Poe, neither of whom are blest with Dän's unequivocal approval. In their turn Blake and Poe, genuine creators, whatever their failings, are counter-pointed against the East German authors' collective, for whom Dän has nothing but contempt.

A different kind of counterpoint may be seen in a passage on pages 794–5 which describes an exercise of the Bundeswehr, an organization Dän hates with especial fervour. Here the central column divides once again, this time roughly along ideological lines: for on the left we are given the actions and words of characters who either are soldiers or admire soldiers and soldiering, while the right brings us Dän's sardonic commentary to Franziska, together with an explanation of his anti-militaristic and anti-patriotic stance: '2 erlebte Weltkriege, (und die Zeitn drum=rum nich minder) habn Meine Liebe zum Vaterlande wundersam abgekühlt . . .'. Since Dän is the central intelligence, however, the left-hand column's description of the sayings and doings of 'patriots' is shot through with phrases suggesting and describing Dän's attitude towards them ('. . . auch von der MüllitärPest bephall'n. (Wie all=die Mülljardn!)'), while the right-hand column is occasionally 'invaded' by characters that belong to the left-hand one in order to illustrate Dän's commentary. All this while, the margins continue, on both sides, with their task of expanding what is said in the central columns, illustrating it, or suggesting simultaneous actions and sensations.

Three further uses of column-division must claim our attention, however briefly. One of these is to suggest the literary and legendary prefigurations which play such an important part in the structure of Schmidt's novel. Thus on pages 730–1, we have an account of the life of St Frances on the left, while the right has an account of the activities of a modern Frances, the Franziska of the novel, with ironic sidelights on one of Schmidt's *bêtes noires*,

Görres's *Christliche Mystik*. Another, even more important function of parallel columns, is to suggest simultaneously quotidian reality, and the fantasies which take off from it. A clear example occurs on page 755:

> (Sie vertraute mir Ihr Händlein so=Fröl' ich an:!
>
> :" 'ch hab sô=wahnsinnich lach^{ch}n müssn   /(InMir entstand dies=Bild:
> —: (muth Mein Gesicht dann=ma ausruhn)   obm=Mein Schreibtisch. Lin
>
> —" (Sie verfl$^{o}_{u}$chte Meine Hand zärtlinger   ks, unterm DachFenster, Fr'
> in=Ihre:—):" — das hatt'ch Ma schonn ge   s Lager;) 'Ihr "betten" dürfn.
> $\frac{dacht}{hofft}$, dass Du *die*=Oll'n nich gemocht   (Köpfel, wo jetz ZT liegt.))
> hassD . . .   ; Füsse in der eckstn=Ecke...
>   (((einer schwarzn NacktSchnecke ausweichn)))

This is a simple example of a technique Arno Schmidt used more elaborately in his novel *KAFF auch Mare Crisium*. What he calls LG, or *Längeres Gedankenspiel* — the fantasies that take off from the actualities of our life — are a constant theme of his critical and essayistic work as well as his fiction.[7] In a way the whole of *Zettel's Traum*, with its dream of a young girl in love with a crabbed aging writer, may be seen as the extended LG of the man who created Dän and then credited him with the authorship of works which figure, in our library catalogues, under the name of Arno Schmidt. Again and again the work invites us to draw biographical inferences: by precept (does Dän not speak of books as 'geistije Aktaufnahm' des Verfassers, mit Selbstauslöser' on page 1213?) and by presenting as elements in Dän's biography facts that fit Arno Schmidt's. In a way the book teases us to do for Schmidt what Dän does for Poe — with the implication, however, that the self-aware twentieth-century writer has done the job of self-exposition consciously and thoroughly, and cannot, therefore, be 'caught out' in the way Dän seeks to 'catch out' Poe.[8]

One last example of column-division, and we have done with it. On page 1311 the central block of print divides in the way now familiar to us, while the glosses continue on both sides. The left-hand column so formed evokes Wilma amusing herself in the bath-tub; the right-hand column has Franziska and Dän, themselves unseen, watching Wilma's antics:

'Sie [i.e. Franziska] legDe den Finger auf den Mund; (=vor'm BadeFenster :!—)/;—?—/ und Fr grinSDe heunisch ;O—: à la 'also dàs muss man ja geseh'n habm!'

Here the splitting of the central column evokes a *voyeur* situation. The watchers are on the right, the watched is on the left; but since what the watchers see enters their minds to be reflected on, at least one of Wilma's actions is described in the right-hand margins, on the watchers' side. The function of the split column is once again that of evoking two simultaneous and related happenings.

Similar effects can be produced by manipulations of syntax. Take Dän's characteristic pronouncement: 'Ich bin nicht (weder gekommen noch) da?: die Kindlein zu lehren' (1106). That conflates, or superimposes, no less than four different constructions: 'Ich bin nicht da, die Kindlein zu lehren'; 'Ich bin weder gekommen noch da, die Kindlein zu lehren'; 'Bin ich da, die Kindlein zu lehren?'; 'Bin ich gekommen, die Kindlein zu lehren?' — while constituting, at the same time, a parody and denial of New Testament ethics and attitudes. Such conflations are often produced by a device which supplements in a telling way the column division we have already examined. Instead of a vertical line dividing column from column, or, often, in addition to that vertical line, we find a horizontal line dividing word from word or phrase from phrase. A transparent example occurs on page 625:

$$\frac{\text{gelbgraues}}{\text{grüngelbes}} \text{ Licht: } \frac{\text{zucknde Schwüle}}{\text{das grosse Maisfeld}}.$$

That tries to fix a complex impression of light and land-scape. The colour is difficult to describe exactly — the first attempt, 'gelbgrau', has immediately been supplemented by another, 'grüngelb' and the two adjectives therefore occupy the same place in the sentence; one beneath the other instead of one after the other, they both qualify 'Licht'. The next portion of the sentence — if I may use this term for a construction which, though self-contained, lacks a finite verb — is again made up of two elements not lineally consecutive but standing one on top of the other, divided by a horizontal line in the manner of a common fraction in mathematics. This time the superposition tries to convey the simultaneity of two separate sense-impressions — of movement of air and temperature on the one hand (zucknde Schwüle) and of a familiar rural landscape on the other (das grosse Maisfeld). Schmidt makes use of this device for different purposes, but chiefly to convey the contradictory nature of many of our impressions and emotions.

Wilma is said to be $\frac{\text{hingerissn}}{\text{ungehaltn}}$ (p. 605); Poe-scholars

contemplate their findings $\frac{\text{betrübt}}{\text{erfreut}}$ (p. 679); Franziska

'taumlte, halb $\frac{\text{singend}}{\text{weinend}}$ von Fenster zu Fenster' (p. 732);

and one minor character reports of another of whom he cannot tell for certain whether her illnesses are genuine, imaginary or shammed: 'Se $\frac{\text{iss}}{\text{tut}}$ nämich immer "leidnd" ' (p. 804). Sometimes the device is exploited for a kind of surface translation-effect, English 'my dear' above the horizontal line becoming grandiloquent archaic German below it: 'Maid Dir' (p. 834). This instance is particularly interesting and important, for it shows clearly the polyglot resonances Dän and Arno Schmidt seek to detect in our simplest utterances.

Nor is it only complete phrases or complete words which are taken out of the lineal forward flow of the narrative by this superpositioning device borrowed (like much else in *Zettel's Traum*) from mathematics. By presenting alternatives for just a few letters, or even just one letter, within a single word, Schmidt can make us aware of two simultaneous reactions or emotions: as when the last two syllables of the word 'angewidert' are moved up, above a horizontal line, beneath which appears the alternative syllable 'regt', so that we have the immediate impression that the characters are in a state in which readers of *Zettel's Traum* will also frequently find themselves: 'ange $\dfrac{\text{widert}}{\text{regt}}$ ' (p. 785). If a character is present in body but absent in mind, Schmidt calls him 'den A$\frac{\text{n}}{\text{b}}$wesendn' (p. 83); he evokes simultaneously truth and illusion, 'wahr' and 'wahn', by placing the letter 'r' above and the letter 'n' below a horizontal line in the phrase 'eine (wah$\frac{\text{r}}{\text{n}}$haft cgjungsche!) Bedeut-ung' (p. 677) — which also tells us something of Dän's ambivalent feelings about Jung's theories. Similar effects can be produced by the use of brackets. By bracketing the letter 'e' in the word 'verseucht', Dän can charac-terize the writer as a man at once 'tempted' by words and 'infected' by them: 'ein wortvers(e)uchtes Individuum; gestraft damit, Nährbottom für Etyms zu sein' (p. 393).

Brackets and superpositioning work together in Dän's arrangements for his literary remains: 'daß nûr ein(e) not$\frac{o}{a}$rische(r) Nicht-Christ(in) Mein'n Nachlass $\frac{verwal}{auswer}$ tn dürfn solle' (p. 1284).

Dän's characterization of the writer, quoted a moment ago, referred to a device which is more fully exploited in *Zettel's Traum* than any other: those elaborate puns and telescopings which Lewis Carroll has called 'portmanteau words', Joyce 'perfiguring', and Schmidt 'Etyms'. Unconsciously, Schmidt believes, we all make use of these, to whisper secret things beneath 'harmless' or exalted utterances; it should be the artist's task to use them consciously, in order to portray psychological complexities, to expose pretentiousness and self-deception, and to play wittily with language and with the world that our language attempts to describe and control. The term 'Etyms' is, of course, an abbreviation of 'Etymologien'.[9] Such 'Etyms' are often polyglot: it is easier to speak of embarrassing things in a language not your own, writers worth their salt tend to be polyglot anyway, and the more languages you allow yourself to play with, the more double and triple meanings you will be able to convey in the words you use. Paul, therefore, is made to define the use of 'Etyms' as 'eine durable Technik des unendlich=klein=Polyglotten . . . im Vergleich zu der die bisherigen "Worte" allmählich "einsprachig" zu wirken hätten' (p. 28); Wilma mocks at Dän's 'krypto-akustische Künste' (p. 323); and Dän himself is allowed his most lyrical flight in praise of this device, characterizing the 'Etym' as

Eine wandlnde Blume. Ein dem (Wort=Zweig) entblühter Vogl, Ein mit feurijn Funkn leuchtnder (Buchstabm=) SpringBorn. Ein (Sinn=)singendes Reis.   (p. 1027)

In order to make words more transparent, more capable
of combining with other words in a game of double and
triple meanings across several languages, Schmidt has
adopted a system of spelling which ignores all the Duden
rules, bypasses the international phonetic alphabet, yet
manages admirably to convey the sounds and rhythms
of modern German with various Silesian and North
German dialect peculiarities.

Two uses of the 'Etym'-method must, however, be
strictly distinguished if we are to do justice to Schmidt's
achievement. The first of these is described by Dän in
the following way:

'Ich erlaub Mir, dem Herrn, an praktischn Beispieln, die
Etym=Methode zu demonstriern ... Ein (allerdings kom-
pliz'iertes) Verfahren der TextUntersuchung; aufgebaut auf
BuchstabmVerschreibbarkeiten einer=, auf statistischen Häuf-
ungen von starren Bilderfolgn andererseits ...' (p. 1064)

Dän tries, in other words, through an examination of
possible double meanings and revealing image-sequences,
to get at the 'real' content of the writings of what he calls
DP's: 'Dichter-Propheten', men who think they are
proclaiming some uplifting message while in reality their
work speaks, to the adverted ear, of humbler physical
needs and longings which their consciousness has repressed. The chief object of demonstration in *Zettel's
Traum* is the work of Edgar Allan Poe. Dän will look at
some extract from one of Poe's writings — at, let us say,
Poe's review of Dickens's *Old Curiosity Shop*. He will
then quote an innocent-looking fragment, with some
deformations of spelling. Say that Poe describes 'the
glorious scene, where the man of the forge sits poring, at
deep midnight, into that dread fire', and then goes on to
speak of 'the whole conception of his character' and to

mention 'a simple denizen of the earth'. In *Zettel's Traum*, the word 'whole' (in 'the whole conception') is spelt h-o-l-e, just as throughout the book the German noun 'Fall' (in, say, 'auf jeden Fall') is spelt 'P-h-a-l-l'; while the English word 'earth', I regret to report, is deformed to 'a-r-s-e' (p. 977). Dän somewhere adduces the Marlowe Society's Shakespeare recordings as warrant for that last deformation; but like several other such distortions, it suggests to an English ear nothing so much as the speech of a drunk with a thick German accent. Having 'quoted' Poe in this form, Dän then proceeds, to the admiring astonishment of Paul and Franziska and amid feeble protests from Wilma, to read scatological meanings into the passage, meanings, we are to believe, hidden from Poe himself, indicative of secret desires and repressed memories. In the passage from the *Old Curiosity Shop* review, Dän's auditors are told to believe, 'scene' hides 's-e-e-n', what the voyeur wishes he had done; forge suggests 'furnace' which in its turn suggests 'fornicare' plus 'fur-niche'; 'whole' is 'h-o-l-e' and goes, in meaning, with the first syllable of 'con-ception' and, indeed, with the whole secondary meaning of that word — 'con-ception is a blessing, but not as your daughter may conceive'.

Der hockt also, once upon a midnight dreary; und gafft in'ne fur=niche (die jedoch 'grauses Feuer' birgt, dh 'verbrannt' ist & verbrennen=kann!); 'S iss ebm ne 'hole=con'sception. (p. 977)

This is just one typical example of something that goes on throughout *Zettel's Traum*. Unconvincing in most cases, this application of the 'Etym' method soon becomes exceedingly wearisome; its unremitting pursuit consti-tutes the most serious flaw in the work, and makes us doubt the sanity of Dän and those who so readily agree with him rather than that of Poe. That Poe has his problems ('Der andauernd Katzen die Augen ausbohrt, Leute lebendich einmauert, oder Seine Helden Sich gegenseitich verzehren lässt — : *und* darüber dithyrambisch, im Höheren Ton, berichtet' — p. 381) — that we knew already. Few readers will agree, however, that the play with sexual and excretory double entendre in which Dän indulges throughout *Zettel's Traum* makes Poe's text 'interessanter & witzijer' (p. 1154): a little goes a very long way, and acute boredom soon supervenes. A lot of it is self-parody, no doubt, and parody of the *Sex-Welle* to boot; but this defeats itself in the end, leading to boredom and the temptation to skip.

Happily, however, the search for scatological double meanings in the work of humourless poets — DP's, Dän calls them, 'Dichter-Priester', 'displaced persons', 'deplazierte Perönlichkeiten', 'dignes de pitié' — is not the only way in which the 'Etym' method is used in *Zettel's Traum*. It is much more effective when it suggests mental processes in Dän himself, or gives a complicated statement its most concentrated form. 'Sünd alle von Eddyms Kindern', it flashes through Dän's mind (p. 213): we are all sinful humans, children of Adam; we are all the children of 'Eddy', of Edgar Poe — he has influenced, or prefigured, us all; we are the children of 'Etyms', of etymologizing word-play. The last is, of course, literally true of the characters in the book, whose names have been selected to lend themselves to various kinds of play: Wilma — willma(l), Fränze — frenzy, Paul — Poel... The hero's name especially, is a 'speaking' name — Daniel, the man in the fiery furnace or the lions' den who interprets dreams and understands the writing on the wall; Pagenstecher, a Westphalian name one of whose connotations may be 'gadfly' or 'hornet';[10] Daniel Pagenstecher, the man whose initials — irony of ironies! — are those of the 'DP's' on whom he so looks down.

Etyms are also used, with happy results, as a means of satire; as a means, above all, of characterizing things, conveying an attitude to things, while pretending merely to name them. We have already met Dän's reference to the East German 'authors' collective' — an appellation he spells in such a way that it suggests pain (Au)[11] at such authors' folly (Thoren), their brown-nosing (Cullec . . .) and the depths to which they have sunk (tief) (p. 1166). Almost every page will yield similar examples. A girl-chasing soldier is called 'ein junger Bundeswerwolf'. A camp-follower of the *Bundeswehr* appears, in *Zettel's Traum*, as a 'pulligame Schäferin'; here Schmidt has merged the 'Pulli' that emphasizes the girl's curves with 'polygamy' and with the old 'game' in which she is engaged, while evoking, at the same time, a contrasting pastoral idyll whose negative co-presence can be felt again and again throughout *Zettel's Traum*.

The pattern of division and fusion presented by the technical devices I have been analysing is the formal reflection of Schmidt's thematic concern with what he calls *Zerlegung*. One female character is made to complain of this in society: 'die MenschnMännchen scheinen sich (verhängnisfoll!) "zerlegt" zu habm. In "Gewicht-Heber" stämmhaftester Sorte; ? ; & in, (phil'i'crannychSDe!) Gedankn-Spieler' (p. 1025). Dän himself is said to be, by the perceptive Paul, 'immer=eigen —: "zerlegt" möcht' Ich sagn; stet'S nur halb=da, (obwohl diese Deine l=Hälfde für de Menschn vollstänDich genügte; (die andre moitié war grundsätzlich im Bereich etwelcher Werke-))' (pp. 1020–1). Such inner division within the

12

artist brings in its train the kind of division of the objects
of love which is familiar to all readers of E. T. A. Hoffmann, whose *Der goldne Topf* is one of the many literary
works to which the Dän–Franziska plot is consciously
related. In a characteristic variation on Hoffmann's
pattern of 'aesthetic idol' and bourgeois beloved Dän
speaks of a resolute division, 'eine resolute "Zerlegung",
eine "Auseinanderschiebung"', of the sexual drives:
'für den Äther ein (präraffaelitisch=) feines LG=Bräut
$\frac{\text{lein}}{\text{igam}}$; ... — ...: für den $\frac{SW}{SV}$ amp=untn,[12] Was absichtlich
Erniedrüchtes=Freches' (p. 1139). Explaining this
'Unterschied von "himmlischer" und "irdischer"
Libido' to Franziska, Dän describes how, within the
human personality, 'das "Untere Ende" sich den Kuttl-
SchmerBauch streicht & höhn'nd hinauf=rülpSd —:
zum "Oberen Ende"; das, seinerseits, das Thierische
unbehaglich bemitleidet ...: womit ja gleich eine Zerlegung der Persönlichkeit in mehrere "Instanzen" be-
gründet & angebahnt iss!' (p. 1138).

The view of the human personality implicit in that last
sentence clearly derives from that of Freud. Dän recognizes,
as three of his 'Instanzen', the Freudian Unconscious, Ego
and Super-Ego; but he adds to this what he calls 'die
vierte Instanz', discerned in certain favoured individuals
of fifty or more, in whom the sexual drives have lost some
of their former power, and whom disillusion with parents,
teachers, political leaders and boyhood heroes have led
to look with a sceptical eye at the demands of the Super-
Ego. This 'vierte Instanz' is the liberating faculty of
seeing through the games played by the Unconscious and
the Super-Ego at the expense of our own Ego and that
of others. In a work like *Finnegans Wake*, therefore, we
are enabled to hear at once:

die '4 Stimmen' . . . Das TriebGeröchl des ubw; den starr=
sterilen Tadl des ÜI; das commishaft=überforderte Mit=
N$_u^o$ttiern des Ich; und endlich das HerrlichSDe, das hell=zer-
sprungen klirrende Gelechta der 4. Instanz. (p. 916)

This rare faculty allies itself with the Ego, laughs at the
Super-Ego and comes to terms in a special way with the
Unconscious; and Dän's description of this process constitutes an explanation and justification of the language
of *Zettel's Traum*, its playing with double meanings and
portmanteau words:

Sie [i.e.: 'die 4. Instanz'] entzieht dem ubw grosse Energie-
beträge; und bemächticht sich dessn StummlSprache — man
kann sich also jetz mit diesm Caliban verständijn; ja, den
unbeholfnen Wilden verspottn; und der wird sogar wider-
strebend überlistigt werdn: hört er doch seine plumpsche
Redeweise reizend=verfeinert und beiphallgewinnend sch-
watzn. (p. 916)

The result is said to be analogous to a vocal quartet, like
'Bella figlia dell' amore' in *Rigoletto*:

ein 'Quartett' . . . (meinethalbm ooch n Tetralog;) zwischn den
4 Instanzn . . . 'DoppelDuett' wäre noch=präziser; auf jeder
Seite 2* Pärchen: das dumpf=wollustgurrglnde ubw & das
giftich=magistrale ÜI? —: contra ein, die AussnWelt beo-
bachtn (& reagieren)müssndes Ich; ab 50 erleichtert=vereint
mit einer souverän=geistreich=lächernDän 4. Instanz. (p.914)

The parelleling and superimposing devices we have been
examining help to give just this effect of many voices
sounding together within one human personality. Poe's
writings are brought in as a contrast, for they are said to
lack the fourth voice; in them we are to watch an Ego
directed by two forces stronger than it: 'Das ÜI bedient

---

* Dän means *one* pair on each side: only four 'Instanzen' are involved.

12*

sich der korrektn NormSprache; das ubw lüstert, etymsch, hinein' (p. 909). Here another type of 'Zerlegung' is indicated: the activity of the literary demythologist who can show up, and laugh at, the tricks played by the tyrants above and below; who can free the human consciousness, temporarily at least, within the confines of a work of art that is at once analysis and synthesis, from the three pressures to which it is constantly subjected:

die lebmsgefährliche Aussnwelt; der Drüsenterror des ubw; das pausenlose sterile Getadele Dessn, was bestnfalls die Repräsentanz der Normalität sein kann.   (p. 913)

The constant discussions of Poe serve, therefore, as yet another counterpointing device.

It may well be thought — as I have already suggested — that a character like Dän is ill-equipped to liberate anybody from anything. The shrillness of his attacks on those who do not share his opinions, his unremitting attempts to read sexual meanings into everything, his bouts of self-pity, his self-admiration, his urge to withdraw and hide coupled with an incessant desire to monologize, — all these suggest psychological disturbances as serious as any of those he attributes to Poe. What is even more disquieting is the indulgence with which Arno Schmidt treats this creation: the way he allows him to hold forth uninterrupted to admiring auditors, while the one character who occasionally disagrees — Wilma — turns out to be a stupid, unconsciously cruel, sex-ridden ex-Nazi. Yet Schmidt does ask us to believe that his Dän has achieved insights denied to the generality of mankind, and that for these insights he has had to pay a price. He is, inescapably, an intellectual, a brain-animal, a *voyeur* who watches other people enjoy themselves while he is himself all but impotent. He is a 'verkrusteter Sonderling' (p. 869), a 'literarischer Stachanow' (p. 996), afflicted with the itch to pry into the secret activities of others in order to convert these into literature. Again the 'man of 50' theme obtrudes itself: 'Die zunehmende Bedeutung der SchauLust?: iss der Ausdruck eingeschränkter S=Aktivität: an die Stelle rüstijer S=Leistung tritt der Hang zum tatnlosn V aus der Ferne' (p. 1327). Artists have a peculiar kinship with the *voyeur* — one of Dän's glosses on Poe speaks, significantly, of 'gewisse Klassen von Geistern (Intellek-tuellen?), sonst auch Voyeure genannt' (p. 1067). One does not have to read far in *Zettel's Traum*, or anywhere in Schmidt's later work, to find an obsessional concern with the voyeur and what he sees — a notable instance is the short story *Caliban über Setebos*, which has many thematic and stylistic links with *Zettel's Traum*; and we have already seen how the split-column technique is used, in *Zettel's Traum*, to mirror and mimic the relation-ship between watcher and watched. That Schmidt is not the only modern writer who finds this theme attractive would not be difficult to demonstrate — one of the novels of Alain Robbe-Grillet is, we remember, actually entitled *Le Voyeur*.

There are, however, voyeurs and voyeurs, and some, we are meant to believe, are more contemptible than others. There are, for one thing, those who know what they are doing and why, and those who do not; those who laughingly accept the weaknesses of their minds and flesh, and those who disguise them, from themselves as well as others, presenting them as something nobler than they are. The work of Edgar Allan Poe serves, in *Zettel's Traum*, as an instance of such penetrable disguise. As Paul says, after Dän's interminable Poe-analyses have

convinced him more thoroughly than they will most
readers, however open-minded these readers may be:

Der Kerl (der POE) schwaddronirt doch tatsächlich, Wort für
Wort, bloss immer vom VoyeurGlück! Nich dass ich was
dagegn hätte; aber es iss (Dän hat Recht) ne Zumutung,
wenn er Mir das als ErkenntnisTheorie uffschwatzn will: Sein
lachhafter Mangel anSelbstEinsicht deklassiert ihn.   (p. 1267)

Yet whatever his failings — due, in the last analysis, to
the lack of a 'vierte Instanz' in his psychic make-up —
Poe is still an artist, still to be respected for his constant
endeavours to transmute the dross of his inner and outer
life into art. He has little in common with those 'watchers'
for whom Dän reserves his greatest contempt: the
Tele-Voyeur (p. 1171) of modern times. Television per-
formances are characterized by Dän as 'Modernster
Anleit zur Voyeurereye, all diese Film=& Fernseh-
Nickel; (in effigie pimpern; dazu Vorhänge=vor &
verfinstert . . .)'. Himself a habitual if selective TV
watcher, Dän has the heartiest contempt for its hypno-
tized mass-audience; a contempt he shares — as many
essays and obiter dicta demonstrate — with Arno
Schmidt.

Television is only one of many media that bombard
modern man with information; even the quiet air of the
countryside, to which Dän has fled from the cities in which
most of his readers live, is transformed by the transistor-
radio into 'schwatznde Lüfte' (p. 534). Nor can anyone
escape from the constant intrusion of advertisements.
Here again the techniques Schmidt has evolved justify
their existence. The reproduction of actual advertisements in the margins represent the unavoidable intrusion
of such material into even the most jealously guarded
privacy, while at the same time 'estranging' it sufficiently,

by the de-commercialized context in which it now
appears, to make it amusing. Parallel-column, marginal
gloss and 'portmanteau' devices, for their part, are well
adapted to represent the Babel of conflicting voices from
West and East, and to show what happens when all this
'information' comes up against a mind stuffed with
reminiscences of a wide variety of authors and pursuing,
or trying to pursue, its own lines of thought.

In discussing the relation between the main themes of
Zettel's Traum and its sometimes apparently eccentric
stylistic devices, we have had to glance more than once
at its use of literary allusion. The function of the Poe
analyses in particular should, by now, have become clear.
They represent, first of all, a concrete instance of Dän's
passionate involvement with literature — the involvement of a man who feels uncomfortable in his society:
'Für mich', says Dän, 'gibt es nur l-Heimat; nämlich
die=Literatur', adding, characteristically: 'und die iss
man ooch noch so-so' (p. 471). At the same time, however, Dän is credited with a constant desire to get beyond
aesthetic contemplation, to penetrate through the story
or poem to the life of the artist: 'aus der bloßn "Literatur"
in eine Meta=Literatur zu gelangen' (p. 510). This
enterprise is possible because he believes himself to have
recognized 'wie sich, im Werk eines Künstlers, zwangs-
läufich, auch sein Lebm & Treibm mit=abbildn müssn:
allso wird auch seine Triebausrichtung, dänn und
wonn, einsickern=durchschlagn=sichtbarwerdn. Und nun
ebm *nìcht* als dürre Definition; wohl aber als über-
zeugnde, nächtigst=huschnde Gestalt' (p. 509). Thus
discerned, Poe's life supplies parallels, some openly
discussed, some only implied, with the lives of the
characters who appear in *Zettel's Traum*. The voyeurism
and sexual difficulties attributed to him play a part in

Dän's life too; Poe's marriage to his child-bride suggests the Franziska–Dän relationship; his drinking-problem is shared by his translator Paul (whose name is occasionally conflated with Poe's to make 'Poel'); above all, he is, like Dän, a writer of fiction and therefore faced with the perennial difficulties that confront such writers. Asked why he spends so much time and energy on analysing Poe's work and relating it to Poe's life, Dän answers: '(Weil Er=für=Mich l Staffl darstellt): "in der ErCunntnis der MöchtIchkeiten des KühnSteLeyerManns" ' (p. 1068) — a portmanteau statement which suggests at once the artist's sexuality, Utopian longings, desire for self-aggrandisement, power, boldness, poverty, lack of social integration and obsessive monotonous concern with a few central themes. Poe's enterprise, as Dän presents it, is that which he imputes to every great artist: transmuting the indignities and the dross of our physical life — indignities and dross on which *Zettel's Traum* dwells almost literally *ad nauseam* — transmuting these into a work of art which can give aesthetic delight. But though in one way Poe stands for the artist *tout court*, in another he represents only one possible stage, 'Staffl', of artistic development; for he has not attained the self-knowledge and insight Dän attributes to 'die vierte Instanz'. He writes stories and poems that can powerfully affect you, especially when you are young,[13] but to a maturer insight a shoddiness appears in his work which Dän attributes to the combined operations of a vengeful Unconscious, an ingrown Super-Ego, and an Ego that loses artistic control. Poe's life and work therefore provide both parallels and contrasts to those of the fictive writer into whose consciousness *Zettel's Traum* transports us, and Dän's constant analyses are to be treated 'als Denkmodell, als logisch=überstrenges' (p. 1080); a 'model' illustrating the dangers, difficulties and possibilities of transmuting life into art.

Among the thousands of allusions to other literary works which crowd the pages of *Zettel's Traum* one set claims our particular attention: that suggested by the title of the book, and by its epigraph.

I have had a most rare vision. I have had a dream, — past the wit of man to say what dream it was: man is but an ass, if he go about to expound this dream. Methought I was — there is no man can tell what. Methought I was, and methought I had, — but man is but a patch'd fool, if he will offer to say what methought I had. The eye of man hath not heard, the ear of man hath not seen, man's hand is not able to taste, his tongue to conceive, nor his heart to report, what my dream was.

'Zettel', German for the 'warp' of woven cloth, is the name under which Bottom the weaver appears in Schlegel's translation of *A Midsummer Night's Dream*. Other meanings of 'Zettel' are also relevant; thousands of index-cards and scraps of paper, arranged in *Zettelkästen*, went to the making of *Zettel's Traum*, thus placing the scholar's methods in the service of a dream — 'Bei uns Intellektollen träumt das Denken' (p. 1127). Wilma actually speaks of *Zettelkasten=Krämer* on page 114, and each separate page of the book is headed '*zettel*' followed by a number. Title and epigraph, however, refer as unmistakably to *A Midsummer Night's Dream* as the title of Joyce's *Ulysses* does to the Odyssey.

Just as the Poe discussions and quotations are justified by a *donnée* of the plot (Paul has secured a publisher's commission to translate Poe and is enlisting Dän's help), so the *Midsummer Night's Dream* too justifies its place in the characters' consciousness by such reminders as hearing the Mendelssohn wedding march played over the radio; by reminiscences of a performance of the play with the inimitable Helmut Qualtinger as Bottom; and by the fact that Paul, Wilma, and Franziska have recently been listening to a gramophone recording of the whole play which so impressed Franziska that she has learned large chunks of the *Midsummer Night's Dream* by heart. Franziska is therefore able to join in the game of (usually punning) allusions played by Dän, who is gifted with an extraordinarily ready, accurate and extensive verbal memory.

When Franziska shows that she is physically as well as mentally attracted to him, Dän, who has a low opinion of his own physical charm and powers, at once casts himself as Bottom wooed by Titania. Their *LG à deux*, fantasies of a possible life together, therefore becomes 'Bottom's dream' — 'it shall be called Bottom's dream, because it hath no bottom' — and is accompanied, throughout the book, in marginal glosses and main text, by direct quotations from the exchanges between the transmogrified Bottom and the infatuated fairy-queen. ' "Thou art as wise as thou art beautiful!" (Not so neither, Du)' (p. 212). ' "So is mine eye enthralled to thy shape!" 'Methinks, mistress, you should have little reason for that' (p. 485). At the same time other facets of the *Midsummer Night's Dream* come into play: Franziska casts herself as Helena spurned by Demetrius ('Dän-Metrius'), Dän sees her, in her more mischievous moods, as Puck, in her more ethereal, childish and ministering aspects as Peaseblossom or Cobweb, and once she is even made to speak 'in a monstrous little voice' like Bottom himself. Dän plays his one self-assumed part throughout, but he does not remain merely Bottom the ass in Titania's arms. Bottom's other sayings and doings come to his mind as he goes through his day: 'My chief humour is for a tyrant'; 'Thisby, the flowers of odious savours sweet' (the combination of odorousness, sweetness, odiousness and love preoccupies Dän continually); 'Find out moonshine, find out moonshine' and so on.

The *Midsummer Night's Dream* is not exempt from Dän's tendency to play sexualizing etymological games; and indeed, as cabaret and music-hall comedians have always known, the names of the characters in Shakespeare's comedy (especially those of Bottom and Titania) lend themselves to jokes of this kind. At the same time our own age has become peculiarly alive to sexual implications in *A Midsummer Night's Dream* which were hidden to an earlier generation of readers and playgoers — implications brought out particularly clearly in Peter Brook's production seen in Stratford in 1970 and in London in 1971. After Jan Kott and Peter Brook, we should be well prepared to accept Dän's stress on the sexual side of Titania's relationship to Bottom the ass, and should not be shocked too much by his punning distortions of Shakespeare's text.

In Dän's mind, and in the minds of the other characters, *A Midsummer Night's Dream* associates itself with other literary works. All reading brings with it a network of such relationships. Chief among them are associations with Fouqué's *Undine*, which also tells us of the love of an elemental sprite for a mortal, and *Tom der Reimer*, the ballad which shows a *poet's* succumbing to supernatural enchantments. Translated Bottom in the arms of Titania merges with enchanted Tom lured by his 'Elfenkönigin'; and, half-ironically, half-wistfully, Dän sees himself prefigured in both. And as Horst Denkler has reminded us in the most intelligent essay so far published on *Zettel's Traum*: 'Bottom' translates into German 'Po', thus linking Dän=Zettel once again to the ubiquitous Edgar Allan Poe.[14]

Supplemented and enriched by other literary associations, Shakespeare's *A Midsummer Night's Dream*, with its
mingling of magic enchantment, psychological penetra-
tion, overt concern with poetry and poets, and comedy,
presents itself as a counterpoint through out *Zettel's Traum*.
Here too, as so often, we find contrast as important as
parallel. Dän is clearly a much more self-conscious and
self-aware character than the transmogrified Bottom
whose part he playfully assumes; and the world through
which we see him move is more prosaic than the fairy-
haunted woods of Athens. Arno Schmidt often plays
deliberately on such contrasts: as when Franziska reveals
to Dän some particularly sordid details of her parents'
love-life, while the margin quotes Theseus's 'Fair lovers,
you are fortunately met' (p. 1139) or when Dän sees the
drunken Paul off to bed while the margin mocks:
'Lovers to bed! 'tis almost fairy-time' (p. 1287).

As the book nears it end, as night falls on the characters whose adventures we have been following, allusions
to the *Midsummer Night's Dream* become more frequent
and the dream-like atmosphere of the whole becomes
more palpable. The characters are now *living* a 'Midsummer Night's Dream'[15] from which the morning will
bring disenchantment. It is at this point that the meaning
of Bottom's 'translation' subtly changes in the context of
Zettel's Traum. It is still an exhibit in what Schmidt has
called his 'pornografisch[es] Lachkabinett' (p. 915): it
shows up the force which can make an ethereal being
love a braying hairy animal: 'Titania phällt uff'n flätz-
zichstn Weber=Esl rein' (p. 1129), says Paul. It can still
symbolize the strange union of mind and body, dream
and action:

(?—: ZETTEL's Träumungn?); (Unsere Meinungn=&=
Worte *können* der GeisterTail an Uns sein; (Uns're Handlungin

?—: sind immer der Erdn=('untere', 'Körper')=Tail . . .)))
(p. 1140)

Now, however, the power of fairy-enchantment exemplified in Bottom's 'dream' symbolizes also the power of
human arts and sciences to transform life. 'Verwand-
lungsFee'ichkeit' is Dän's punning term for the capability
of the coarse stuff of life to be enchanted, transformed,
ennobled:

Unsre Kultur beruht (anscheinend) auf dieser Verwandlungs-
Fee'ichkeit des S in CunSt= & =WiSSenschaft: etwas, mit dem
'GOtt', scheint's, nich=gerechnet hat. (p. 1159)

This is an elfin transformation different from Bottom's
yet related to it; and Dän refers it to his neo-Freudian
psychology by suggesting, in defence of Poe:

daß wir dem ÜI, am Ende womöglich noch 'dankbar' zu sein
hättn für sein'n 'Druck'? denn nur unter=dém bequem'm
sich doch Unsre 'fancy&imagination' zu jener Elfischn Transformation, die man seitdem Kunst genannt hat . . . zumindest
hat der high=drollic pressure des ÜI zur Entstehung von
'Kunst' außerordntlich beigetragn; (& tut's noch) . . . (p. 1074)

One of the chief monuments to the power of *that* trans-
formation is of course Shakespeare's *A Midsummer Night's
Dream* itself. Here Poe and Dän agree: more than once
Zettel's Traum quotes Poe's *Letter to B*—:

shade of the immortal Shakespeare! . . . Think of all that's
fairy-like . . . the *Tempest* — the *Midsummer Night's Dream* —
Prospero, Oberon and Titania . . . (p. 1168 — cf. p. 931);

while Dän is made to praise it as a 'wunderbares Gebuilde'
which constitutes one of the *loci amœni*, the 'Aufent-
haltsmöglichkeiten' constructed by poets to enable men
to bear their existence with greater equanimity (p. 664).

As this centrally important example of the *Midsummer Night's Dream* should have shown, the literary allusions which occupy so much space in *Zettel's Traum* are not mere arabesques, but play an essential part in determining the structure and meaning of the work as a whole.

One last aspect of *Zettel's Traum* remains to be considered in our attempt to fathom the purpose of some, at least, of its formal eccentricities. It is an essential part of the over-all effect of the work that its chief character should ever feel — and thus make readers feel — the pressure of the past upon the present.[16] The way this pressure makes itself felt in the work can be gauged very well from the passage on pages 794–5 to which reference has already been made: that which shows Wilma, Franziska and Dän watching members of the *Bundeswehr* on and off duty. The left-hand column, it will be remembered, described in often scabrous detail the doings of the soldiers, accompanied by a commentary from their admirers; here the past is summoned up unconsciously, as it were, through the songs the soldiers sing: 'Reich mit den Schätzen des Orients beladen', 'Hoch lebe Oranie=Transvaal'. Meanwhile the right-hand column gives us Dän's bitter reminiscences of a past that has made him the anti-militarist and despiser of national glory that he now is.

2 erlebte Weltkriege (und die Zeitn drum=rum nich minder) habm Meine Liebe zum Vaterlande wundersam abgekühlt, Franziska!

Or again:

(Was könnt' Ich Alles wissen (bzw geleistet habm), wären nich die ewich=verfluchtn 12 Jahre Hitler=&=milli=tear gewesn! Ma nich=abgeseh'n davon, daß sie uns alle, Männer wie Frauen, zu S=Krüppln & Neurotickern gemacht habm.) (Und das iss ja durch die Generatjôn'n gegangn: Mein Gross-

vater (mütterl.) hatte 64=66=7071 'mitgemacht'; Mein Vater
(sowieso 12=Ender) freiwillich ins 'Baltikum'; (Mich hatt' es
noch am ausgiebichstn erwischen müssn tz!)

Or, on a more wistful note:

Aber das war doch ne Schönezeit=damals, gleich nach '20
(und nach '45=wieder); als Unservolk, nach Niederwerfung
seinerselbst, sich ma, eine Zeitlang, zu keinerlei Taten berufn
fühlte!

The right-hand margin supplements these utterances
with unspoken thoughts of the past, adumbrations of
possible speech-acts that stay in the mind, accompanied,
as always, by literary parallels that flash through Dän's
memory; literary parallels and commentaries that range
from the Bible to Thoreau on Civil Disobedience and the
final portions of Heine's *Deutschland. Ein Wintermärchen*:

(außerdem hat man Mich im Kriege dér=Art gehetzt &
geschundn, dass ich des Todes müde ward; geschweige dänn
Deiner Vaterländeley!). ('DANIEL im FeuerOfn; (oder in der
'Löwn Grube'?))/3 Jahre Norwegn;— 'and all day long we
marched through the dim land, against a rushing wind' . . .)

There are flashes, too, of parallel and simultaneous
characters and events in other parts of the world — the
German soldiers observed are likened to soldiers elsewhere; again in unspoken comment, and therefore again
as a gloss in the right-hand margin:

(Soldatesken, wie se am Kongo als 'europäische Elitetruppe'
rum=fremdnlegionern).

All this issues in the snarl at Wilma towards the end of
the right-hand column:

'endlich ma vergessn', Wilma?: wie denksDu Dir das wohl,
so ein 'ungeschehen machn'? —

Arno Schmidt's literary devices are well calculated to
make us re-experience the persistence of such unpurged

memories in our response to the present; well calculated
also to obviate the dangers diagnosed by Dän when he
speaks to Franziska about the tragic problem of the
Zeitroman:

Schön wär's, wenn es ihn gäbe. Aber Ihr, (die ihr jetzt
richtich=lebendich seid), könnt noch nicht schreibm; (Du
weissD, dass=und=wie das gelernt sein will; s'iss schonn
mühsam!) Und wir, die es leidlich=vermögn? —: Wír
schildern ja imgrunde die Generation *vor* Eurem=Jetzt.
(p. 1213)

Through his technical ingenuities Arno Schmidt conveys
at once Dän's present and his past, at once his impression
of the new generation and the experiences of an earlier
time which have helped to shape that impression.

Nor is it only the *public* past (Hitler's wars, *Blut und
Boden* literature, the abuse of language in official propa-
ganda . . .) which is thus recalled in the midst of the
present; Dän's more private past is also made to flash
before our eyes, including a scene undoubtedly meant to
give the reader a clue to the connexion such diverse
themes as sexuality, punning use of language, growing
old and anti-militarism have assumed in Dän's mind.
This vital reminiscence is introduced (on p. 852) as a
marginal gloss, as a sudden flash triggered off in Dän's
mind by the word 'OmaMeessig' (=*omamässig*, granny-
like) in a conversation given in the main text, the central
block of print. No sooner has this word been uttered,
than the gloss begins: '(&, snäppschottIch, 1 meiner
prä'Sten Erinnerungen: Hamburg, 1917 (?16?)) . . .'. All
this while the main text carries on, unconcerned as it
were, with its conversation about the meaning of Poe's
Lionizing. Here too apparent stylistic eccentricities justify
themselves by their expressive purpose and effect.

Towards the end of *Zettel's Traum*, Dän quotes Moritz August Thümmel's saying that a single walk through a spring-time landscape brings with it more actual and possible impressions than can be described in a man's life-time. Since Thümmel's day, Dän adds, life has become more complicated still: 'Ich bin wáhrlich=nicht für die "teem=work"=Téori der DDR; aber Unser "Häutijer=Tâc", möchde, am=erschöpfinsdn, durch ein SynOptikon von 4 × 5.000 Seitn zu erfassn sein' (p. 1326). Besides illustrating Schmidt's use of the natural multivalences of language — 'Unser "Häutijer Tâc" ' is at once the day Dän and his friends have been spending together and the era in which they, and we, live — this sentence also demonstrates Schmidt's need to find technical means to convey exceedingly complex experiences and mental processes in as concentrated a form as possible. In this quest he is helped by many writers of the past to whom he pays due tribute: by James Joyce and Lewis Carroll; by Rabelais (Wilma speaks, at one point, of Dän's 'pantagrueslije Textblähungn' (p. 784); by Sterne and Smollett; by Gutzkow (inventor of *der Roman des Nebeneinander*); and by many others, from Jean Paul to Raymond Queneau. These are Dän's literary heroes; but the stylistic ingenuities of *Zettel's Traum* also recall, consciously or unconsciously, experiments of our own century which Dän does not mention and which Arno Schmidt's literary criticism tends to belittle or to ignore. One thinks of the Futurists' endeavours to transform succession into *simultaneità*; of Kruchenikh's *sdvig*, verbal 'shifts' designed to liberate the double meanings that lurk in innocent-looking sentences;[17] of the many and varied attempts, made by twentieth-century novelists other than Joyce, to 'musicalize' or 'spatialize' fiction;[18] of 'concrete poetry' with its transformation of words into pictorial images. Arno Schmidt is a bee and not a spider, to use the image Matthew Arnold borrowed from Swift. To be sure, Arnold would not have detected in *Zettel's Traum* much that he would have recognized as sweetness and light, and we too have found that when Dän is made to apply his *grosses Etymoskop* (p. 1175) to the work of other writers and to certain aspects of the life of his times, he is as likely to cloud and distort his specimen as he is to illuminate it and show it up in its true colours. But if we stick with *Zettel's Traum*, we are in the end (as I do hope to have shown) rewarded by a literary experience that is well worth while: experience of a consciously 'anti-classical' work of literature, written by a man who has shown by precept and example 'daß die Manieristn das das Salz der Kunstweltn sind' (p. 610).

REFERENCES

[1] Published in a limited edition by the Goverts/Krüger/Stahlberg Verlag, Frankfurt am Main, 1970. All page references are to this edition.

[2] Both these essays are conveniently reprinted in *Nachrichten von Büchern und Menschen*, Vol. 1, Frankfurt am Main, 1971. The passages quoted appear on pages 7 and 221 to 222.

[3] It has been suggested that '-king' also represents the pinging noise made by the wire-fence as it snaps back into position.

[4] 'Das Schauerfeld oder die Sprache von Tsalal.'

[5] This by no means exhausts the suggestiveness of the gloss '(?: NOAH POKE? (oder fu = ?))', which hides allusions to Poe and to Fouqué — one writer, over-ingenious perhaps, has even seen in it an allusion to Arno Schmidt himself (NOAH = AHNO = ARNO). English readers will not need to be reminded of the various colloquial uses of the verb 'to poke'. (Cf. *Bargfelder Bote. Materialien zum Werk Arno Schmidts*, 1. Lieferung, München, 1972, p. 3).

[6] The transformation of parts of the body or objects of daily use into landscapes is a recurrent theme of Schmidt's critical essays and his fiction.

[7] Various kinds of *LG* or *Längeres Gedankenspiel* are discussed in an essay entitled 'Berechnungen II' in Schmidt's *Rosen und Porree*, Karlsruhe, 1959, pp. 296 ff.

[8] One should, however, respect Arno Schmidt's warning against prying too closely into the lives and private circumstances of *living* authors who have transmuted their experiences and difficulties into art: 'Einem *Lebenden* durch "Enthüllungen" 'sein Dasein auf diesem Narrenstern noch mehr erschweren, wäre gemein, und sei den Revolverblättern überlassen, (oder auch ihm selbst); bei einem längst-toten, jedoch durch Dezennien & Säkula immer fürder wirkenden Künstler ist jegliche Theorie oder Hypothese, die das Werk weiter aufschließt,

sein Zustandekommen besser erklärt, und unbegreifliche Gebilde darin begreiflich macht, nicht nur erlaubt, sondern willkommen.' (*Sitara und der Weg dahin. Eine Studie über Wesen, Werk & Wirkung Karl Mays*, Fischer Bücherei edition, Frankfurt am Main, 1969, p. 248.)

[9] Compare Schmidt's explanation of the 'Etym' method, in the course of an analysis of *Finnegans Wake*, in *Der Triton mit dem Sonnenschirm. Grossbritannische Gemütsergetzungen*, Karlsruhe, 1969, pp. 280–1.

[10] According to Max Gottschald's *Deutsche Namenkunde*, Berlin, 1954. Other meanings suggested by the relevant handbooks are 'horse-butcher' (this is the principal meaning) 'horse-gelder' and 'man who looks after, or who lives near, the fence that keeps the horses in' (and, presumably, keeps out thieves and trespassers). There may be a punning reference to the 'pages' of books.

[11] Another possibility is opened up in Schmidt's essay on Karl Philipp Moritz (*Nachrichten von Büchern und Menschen*, Vol. 1, edn. cit., p. 181): 'heißt "Au=Tor" nicht im Grunde "Wiesen-Narr"?'

[12] Here and elsewhere 'S' stands for 'sex' and its derivatives, 'V' for the activities of the voyeur.

[13] Obiter dicta in several essays as well as in the novels *Brands Haide* and *Die Gelehrtenrepublik* attest Schmidt's admiration of works like *Arthur Gordon Pym*.

[14] Horst Denkler: 'Das heulende Gelächter des Gehirntiers. Vorläufiger Bericht über *Zettel's Traum* von Arno Schmidt', *Basis*, II (1971), p. 253. A further essay by Denkler, announced for publication in *Fünftes Amherster Kolloquium* (Heidelberg, 1972), had not appeared when this paper was completed and read to members of the London Universtity Institute of Germanic Studies on 20 January 1972.

[15] Dieter Stündel has calculated that the action of the book takes place on 11 July 1968 (*Der Spiegel*, 18 October 1971, p. 182).

[16] The time-scheme of Schmidt's earlier novels is ably discussed by Reimer Bull in *Bauformen des Erzählens bei Arno Schmidt. Ein Beitrag zur Poetik der Erzählkunst* (Bonn, 1970).

[17] Compare V. Markov, *Russian Futurism. A History*, London, 1969, pp. 341–8.

[18] Compare 'Spatial Form in Modern Literature', in J. Frank's *The Widening Gyre. Crisis and Mastery in Modern Literature*, Indiana University Press edition, 1968, pp. 3–62.